Michael Drayton Revisited

Twayne's English Authors Series

Arthur F. Kinney, Editor

University of Massachusetts, Amherst

TEAS 476

This portrait of Michael Drayton is reproduced from his *Poems* (1619) with the permission of the Henry E. Huntington Library, San Marino, California.

Michael Drayton Revisited

By Jean R. Brink

Arizona State University

Twayne Publisher • Boston
A Division of G. K. Hall & Co.

Publisher's Note
Michael Drayton Revisited by Jean R. Brink is a timely retrospective of Drayton's life and works, taking into account the scholarship that has surrounded Drayton since 1970, when Twayne Publishers issued *Michael Drayton* by Joseph A. Berthelot. We are pleased to offer this new evaluation of Drayton's achievement.

Michael Drayton Revisited
Jean R. Brink

Copyright 1990 by G. K. Hall & Co.
All rights reserved.
Published by Twayne Publishers
A Division of G. K. Hall & Co.
70 Lincoln Street
Boston, Massachusetts 02111

Copyediting supervised by Barbara Sutton
Book production by Gabrielle B. McDonald
Book design by Barbara Anderson

Typeset in 11 pt. Garamond
by Compositors Corporation, Cedar Rapids, Iowa

Printed on permanent/durable acid-free paper
and bound in the United States of America

First published 1990.
10 9 8 7 6 5 4 3 2 1

Library of Congress Cataloging-in-Publication Data

Brink, J. R.
    Michael Drayton revisited / by Jean R. Brink.
        p.   cm. — (Twayne's English authors series ; TEAS 476)
    ISBN 0–8057–6989–7
    1. Drayton, Michael, 1563–1631—Criticism and interpretation.
I. Title.   II. Series.
PR2258.B7   1990
821'.3—dc20   89–26858
                                                        CIP

Contents

About the Author

Jean R. Brink is professor of English at Arizona State University and director of the Arizona Center for Medieval and Renaissance Studies, a statewide research unit. She received her B.A. from Northwestern University, her M.A. from Harvard University, and her Ph.D. from the University of Wisconsin at Madison. She has held summer fellowships at the Newberry Library, Chicago, and the William Andrews Clark Library, Los Angeles. She has edited *Female Scholars: A Tradition of Learned Women Before 1800* (1980) and has published articles on sixteenth- and seventeenth-century biography and on philosophical poetry as well as essays on Sir John Davies and John Milton. She has coedited *The Politics of Gender in Early Modern Europe* (forthcoming, Sixteenth Century Studies) and *The Computer and the Brain: Perspectives on Human and Artificial Intelligence* (forthcoming, Elsevier). She is currently working on an edition of "Rival Friendship," an anonymous seventeenth-century prose romance.

Editor's Note

Michael Drayton is presently one of the most misunderstood and underval-
ued poets of the English Renaissance. In his own time he was one of the most
widely influential and admired of writers: Ben Jonson likened one of his epic
poems to Homer's; Edward Phillips ranked him just below Spenser and
Sidney; Browne and Burton borrowed from him; John Selden annotated his
work in history; and the antiquary William Fulman reports that at his funeral procession the ranks stretched "from his Lodging (in Fleet Street) almost to Strandbridge." He was buried by his contemporaries in Westminster
Abbey alongside Chaucer and Spenser. What they most admired was
Drayton's sense of national history which led to *Englands Heroicall Epistles*
and the "herculean" *Poly-Olbion*. Jean R. Brink's incisive, provocative, and
deeply revisionary study of Drayton makes a powerful case for his importance
now too: in a compelling argument that draws widely on the "new histori-
cism," she shows how Drayton's sense of history was actually subversive: he
drew portraits of Richard II and Edward II that showed parallels to Elizabeth
I and James I long before his contemporaries made such connections; his
harsh and unflinching honesty, measured in his continual failures at patronage and clientage, marks the increasing power and darkness of his vision. Profoundly influenced himself by classical writers (imitating Homer, Lucan, and
Ovid especially), he attempted to maintain the humanist sense of essen-
tialism in a world of contending political and social factions. Such study led
him to the first important Renaissance definitions of genre. What finally
emerges here is a memorable and sympathetic portrait of a genius whose own
sense of ethics was in constant opposition to his life's ambitions, a battle that
made his own work more forceful even as it became more satiric. Brink's
study is a major step in returning Drayton to the position of authority he
achieved in his own lifetime.

Arthur F. Kinney

Preface

Michael Drayton (1563–1631) was born during the reign of Elizabeth I (1558–1603), composed or revised much of his mature work during the reign of James I (1603–25), and published two folio collections under Charles I (1625–49). In 1675 only slightly less stature was granted to Drayton than to Sir Philip Sidney, Edmund Spenser, and Ben Jonson.[1] Indeed, until the middle of the twentieth century, Drayton held a secure position as a minor poet. In 1947 Mario Praz wittily signaled a change in that position: "in the Elizabethan region Drayton's poetry is certainly the most extensive expanse of flat country . . . but . . . [o]nce we have read the four big volumes of Drayton's verse, we relegate them to the back row of our bookcase, only to be consulted by the curious antiquary."[2] Praz's geographical metaphors make it perfectly clear that he dislikes *Poly-Olbion*, but that he also thinks it is Drayton's representative work. Today Drayton's standing as a poet depends on *Poly-Olbion* and a widely acknowledged masterpiece, "Since ther's no helpe, Come let us kisse and part," a sonnet so good that there have been attempts to claim it for Shakespeare.

Drayton's place in the canon needs revision; we have paid too much attention to his chorographical poem and too little to his satire. *Poly-Olbion* (1612, 1622) has always appealed only to the "curious antiquaries"; it took Drayton four years to find a printer willing to bring out the second part. On the other hand, *Englands Heroicall Epistles* (1597) was more popular than Spenser's *Faerie Queene*; no less than seven editions appeared between 1596 and 1609.

Much of Drayton's seventeenth-century poetry broods over the evils in society. In the elegy "To Master William Browne, Of the evill time," for example, he imagines that the devil has taken a purgative and has voided beasts who repeople England. In poem after poem Drayton deplores the impact of a corrupt patronage system on government and literature. This dark and tormented side of Drayton is difficult to square with the mild, inoffensive image that we absorb from twentieth-century accounts of his life and works.

This study will show that critical approaches to Drayton's work have been colored by a biography that ignores and misconstrues the realities of literary clientage, the relation of poets and patrons. We have not only mistaken the kind of poet Drayton was; we have also severely underestimated his contributions to literary theory and criticism. In 1941 Kathleen Tillotson concluded that a chronological study of Drayton's "whole development" between 1590 and 1630 was needed; this study is intended as a preliminary response to that need.[3]

Chapter 1 critically examines the received biography and places Drayton within an immediate social context in which patronage was important for a poet who did not write for the public theater. Focusing on his laureate ambitions and his early clientage connections, chapter 2 traces these themes in his early experiments with genre. In chapter 3 *Englands Heroicall Epistles*, the work Drayton's contemporaries most appreciated, is reread in the historical context of its first appearance. Drayton's ambivalence about literary clientage and its impact on his Jacobean work is examined in chapter 4. *Poly-Olbion* is assessed in chapter 5 as a statement about the function of humane letters. Chapter 6, focusing on *Idea* (1619), demonstrates his increased critical sophistication in *Poems* (1619). In chapter 7 his two Caroline folio collections (1627 and 1630) are examined; *The Muses Elizium* is reinterpreted as his final statement about the future of public poetry. Chapter 8 evaluates Drayton's legacy as a critic and poet.

All references to Drayton's work are to the standard edition, *The Works of Michael Drayton*, edited by J. William Hebel, Kathleen Tillotson, and Bernard H. Newdigate, 5 vols. (1941; reprint, Oxford: Basil Blackwell for the Shakespeare Head Press, 1961). The 1961 corrected edition includes a revised bibliography by Bent Juel-Jensen.

Because Drayton revised a number of his published poems for his 1619 folio collection, the editors have used the revised 1619 versions as copy texts for the poetry he published between 1597 and 1619; these poems are printed in volume 2 in the order in which they appeared in the 1619 folio, not in the order of their first publication. The earlier versions as well as all prefaces, dedications, and commendatory poems appear as variants in volume 5.

Since this study is organized chronologically and examines poems in relation to the context in which they appeared, the first text is as important as the later revised version. I frequently refer to variants and prefatory material printed with the notes in volume 5 of *Works*, which is cited parenthetically as Tillotson. Likewise, the biography accompanying the standard edition, Bernard Newdigate's *Michael Drayton and His Circle* (1941; reprint, Oxford: Basil Blackwell for the Shakespeare Head Press, 1961), is cited parenthetically as Newdigate. Because a number of Drayton's poems involve complex bibliographical issues, I clarify the textual references near the beginning of each chapter.

While working on this book, which at times seemed likely to become the "Herculean toyle" that Michael Drayton called *Poly-Olbion*, I have received the encouragement, helpful criticism, and friendship of librarians, both young and established scholars, and "the regulars" at the Huntington Library. I would like to thank the College of Arts and Sciences, Arizona State University, for supporting the sabbatical leave that enabled me to complete this manuscript at the Huntington Library. Many bibliographical problems were solved as I tried the patience of the gracious staff of the Rare Book Room, presided over by the inimitable Mary Wright. "The regulars" encouraged me with humor and kindness, including me in an atmosphere that defines ideal collegiality.

Those who read this manuscript deserve special praise for their patience; it has existed in nearly as many states as Drayton's revised poems. To Arthur F. Kinney and Margaret Sullivan I owe special thanks for convincing me that I had to revise my first version organized by genre and my second quasi-chronological version as a fully chronological study. Arthur Kinney has been an exemplary and patient general editor. My thanks to John Doebler, Nancy Gutierrez, and Anne Lake Prescott for commenting on sections and to William Gentrup, Diane Facinelli, Beth Birky, and Christopher Burawa for checking clarity and consistency of references. My principal debt is to Dan Brink, who reads drafts only under duress, makes batch files work, and supervises every project I undertake.

Jean R. Brink

Arizona State University

Chronology

1563   Michael Drayton born at Hartshill, Warwickshire.

1580   In the service of Thomas Goodere.

1593   *Idea The Shepheards Garland* entered in Stationers' Register (S.R.) 23 April, dedicated to Master Robert Dudley; *Peirs Gaveston* entered 3 December, dedicated to Henry Cavendish, Esq.

1594   *Ideas Mirrour* entered in S.R. 30 May, dedicated to Anthony Cooke, Esq. (d. 1604), his "ever kind Mecaenas"; *Matilda* dedicated to Mistress Lucy Harington (no S.R. entry).

1595   *Endimion and Phoebe* entered in S.R. 12 April with dedicatory sonnet to Lucy Harington, now Lucy Russell, Countess of Bedford.

1596   *Mortimeriados* entered in S.R. 15 April; *Robert of Normandy* entered 31 November.

1597   *Englands Heroicall Epistles* entered in S.R. 12 October; dedicatory epistles to Lucy, Countess of Bedford, and others.

1598   Gives evidence in suit (*Englebert v. Saunders*) 16 August on behalf of Thomas Goodere's widow. Francis Meres mentions in *Palladis Tamia* that Drayton is already at work on *Poly-Olbion*. To *Englands Heroicall Epistles* Drayton adds five new epistles and deletes dedications to William Parker, fourth Baron Monteagle, and Lord Henry Howard.

1598–1602   Collaborates on plays for the Lord Admiral's Men.

1599   Completes *Englands Heroicall Epistles* by adding Geraldine's reply to the Earl of Surrey.

1602   *Englands Heroicall Epistles* is reprinted with *Idea* and the statement "newly corrected"; epistles of Edward the Black Prince and Alice, Countess of Salisbury, are dedicated to Sir Walter Aston. *The Barons Wars. With Englands Heroicall Epistles* entered in S.R. 8 October but not printed until 1603, dedicated to Sir Walter Aston.

1603   James accedes to the throne 24 March. *To the Majestie of King*

James published (no S.R. entry). Drayton serves as esquire to Sir Walter Aston when he becomes a Knight of the Bath.

1604   *The Owle* appears, dedicated to Sir Walter Aston (no S.R. entry).

1606   *Poemes Lyrick and pastorall. Odes, Eglogs, The Man in the Moone* appears, dedicated to Sir Walter Aston (no S.R. entry). Drayton attacks Selena (Lucy, Countess of Bedford) and Olcon (King James); he praises Frances and Anne (Goodere) Rainsford, identifying Anne as Idea; also praises John, Francis, and Elizabeth Beaumont.

1607   *The Legend of Great Cromwell* entered in S.R. 12 October, dedicated "To the Deserving Memorie of my worthy Patron Sir Walter Aston."

1612   *Poly-Olbion*, part 1, entered in S.R. 7 February, dedicated to Prince Henry, with patronage received from Sir Walter Aston warmly mentioned; John Selden's illustrations dated 9 May. Prince Henry dies 6 November.

1619   *Poems by Michael Drayton Esquyer. Collected into one Volume with sondry Peeces inserted never before Imprinted.* Portrait of Drayton by William Hole. Prose dedication to Sir Walter Aston.

1622   *Poly-Olbion*, part 2, entered in S.R. 6 March, dedicated to Charles, Prince of Wales.

1627   *The Battaile of Agincourt* with *The Miseries of Queene Margarite, Nimphidia, The Quest of Cynthia, The Shepheards Sirena, The Moon-Calfe,* and *Elegies upon Sundry Occasions* entered in S.R. 16 April, dedicated to the "Noblest Gentlemen of Great Britain," commendatory poem by Ben Jonson.

1630   *The Muses Elizium* with *Noahs Floud, Moses His Birth and Miracles,* and *David and Goliah* entered in S.R. 6 March, dedicated to Edward, fourth Earl of Dorset, and Mary, Countess of Dorset.

1631   Dies in London 23 December (approximately) and is buried in Westminster Abbey.

Chapter One
Drayton's Life

Michael Drayton lacks a privileged position in the literary canon and has received little attention from twentieth-century scholars. Examining the life and historical context of a minor poet in a literary golden age may appear to some to be extraneous to literary issues. Nevertheless, the questions that we ask about Renaissance literature, if they are to be fully informed, need to reflect knowledge of more than the work of two or three privileged writers. Drayton offers an interesting example of how nonliterary concerns affect the literary canon. In his case a fictionalized biography has profoundly influenced which of his works are read and even shaped the interpretation of those works. Works that did not suit Drayton's fabricated image have been ignored.

A full-length study of Drayton in 1973 illustrates how biography shapes critical inferences and evaluation:

The reason Drayton never became quite so "modern," or at least unmedieval, as Shakespeare and Spenser is perhaps to be found in his origins. He was born in rural Warwickshire in 1563, and a few years later, in the old feudal way, went to serve as a page for the family of a landed gentleman Henry Goodere. In Goodere's country manor Drayton received all his formal education, and as he tells us in the elegy "To Henry Reynolds," formed his taste in poetry around the romances and ballads of England's past. He stayed with the family until manhood. This is wholly unlike the upbringing of Spenser, a London boy with a good grammar-school and university education. Shakespeare, too, though he hailed from Drayton's shire, grew up in dissimilar circumstances; his father was a tradesman in a thriving market town; he was educated in a grammar school, not by a tutor.[1]

Almost no factual sources exist for the life of Michael Drayton (1563–1631), and those that can be verified are not very revealing. In 1748 William Oldys dismissed seventeenth-century biographical notices by Thomas Fuller (1662, 1684), Edward Phillips (1675), and William Winstanley (1684) because all that these authors had contributed to our knowledge of Drayton was a birthplace, a burial site, and a general "character" of his work.[2]

Drayton's received biography is based almost entirely upon myths fictionalized from autobiographical statements in his work and dedications. Bernard Newdigate's *Michael Drayton and His Circle*, the biography published with the standard edition, appeared in 1941, when patronage relationships were assumed to be more intimate than in fact they were.[3] The heightened rhetoric typically used by a client in addressing a patron was interpreted literally.[4] Newdigate assumed that nearly everyone to whom Drayton addressed a dedication had already offered him patronage. Dedications, by themselves, mean little; authors frequently dedicated works to people whom they did not know. Stephen Gosson, ex-playwright turned Puritan cleric, dedicated his attack on poetry to the poet Sir Philip Sidney, who, although Protestant, did not share Gosson's views of poetry.

Patronage pervaded every facet of Renaissance culture from the church to the government, and literary clientage was part, albeit a small part, of this pervasive system. That Drayton depended upon some kind of patronage for his livelihood, except for intermittent employment as a dramatist from 1598 to 1602, seems reasonably certain, but we do not know what services he performed in his patron's household. The pseudomedieval fiction that Drayton played "minstrel" in the household of a series of country families runs counter to what we know about clientage in Renaissance England. This chapter will sort fact from fiction, reconstructing Drayton's social background and fortunes in the clientage system. A revised biography of Drayton will serve as a context for reevaluation of his career and of the kind of poetry he wrote.

The position of a poet, especially a poet like Drayton, who wrote for a courtly audience and favored historical subjects, was complex because his studies of the past could be interpreted as comments on the politics of the present. Of the many poets whose careers began under Elizabeth I (1558–1603), extended through James I (1603–25) and into the reign of Charles I (1625–49), Drayton is the one poet of stature who was never recognized by the crown. Poets who wrote entertainments for the court included Samuel Daniel, Ben Jonson, William Shakespeare, Thomas Campion, John Marston, William Browne, John Fletcher, Thomas Middleton, George Chapman, and Francis Beaumont.

Drayton's early pastorals and sonnets show that he eagerly tried to gain preferment at court. Inexperienced with the patronage system, he learned the poses and pretenses, the "rules of the game," too late. In 1606 he realized that he had lost his bid for favor and fiercely attacked those who controlled court patronage. His career illustrates how the patronage system politicized poetry, adding nuances to his verse that modern critics have missed because Drayton's poems have never been examined chronologically and so many of his works have been interpreted apart from their specific political and social context.

Early Life: The "Gentrification"

Drayton was born in the vicinity of Hartshill village, Mancetter parish, Warwickshire, early in 1563. The only source for stories of Drayton's early years is a passage in a poem that he wrote when he was sixty-four. In "Of Poets and Poesie," an elegy addressed to Henry Reynolds (1627), he reminisces about his youth as "a proper goodly page," and reports that he asked his tutor "what strange kinde of men" poets were (3:226.22–23).[5] His "milde Tutor" directs him in vintage Elizabethan fashion to Latin classics, "*Mantuan, Virgils Eclogues,* and *William Elderton.*" Drayton's account of his education offers no particulars; his tutor could have been anyone from a clergymen who educated promising village children to the master of a grammar school.

In the first serious biographical study of Drayton in 1748 William Oldys ignores Drayton's reference to having served as a "goodly page," dismissing it as a literary flourish. He comments that Drayton himself tells us "that he was very early smitten with the Love of Poetry, insomuch, that when he was but ten Years old, and no farther advanced than in his Accidence, he was very earnest with his School-master to make him a poet. His Master, it seems, indulged his Wish, and made him very early acquainted with the Latin Classics" (Oldys, 3–4). Not until the late nineteenth century was Drayton's allusion to his "milde Tutor" interpreted as a reference to Sir Henry Goodere and used to fictionalize his youth at Polesworth. Not a single seventeenth- or eighteenth-century biography of Drayton mentions the Gooderes. The first editor to interpret the "goodly page" reference as anything other than a literary allusion was John Payne Collier, who argued that Drayton was a page in the household of Sir Walter Devereux because Drayton's first publication was dedicated in 1591 to Lady Jane Devereux, sister-in-law to Sir Walter (vii).[6]

Collier is also the first biographer to mention the Drayton-Goodere connection, and he admits Goodere as a possible patron, but dismisses any closer connection on the grounds that nothing is heard of the Goodere family in Drayton's work before 1597 (Collier, xxx). Drayton's sheltered youth at Polesworth was invented by Oliver Elton in 1895 and subsequently influenced the *Dictionary of National Biography* article written by A. H. Bullen: "By some chance, or through the brightness of his parts, Michael Drayton, while yet a little boy, was picked out and made a man of by a house of gentle-folk in the same countryside."[7]

When Oliver Elton wrote his *Introduction to Michael Drayton,* a genteel background and a university education were more important credentials than they are today; these marks of respectability may even have been more impor-tant in late nineteenth-century Oxford and Cambridge than they were in Shakespeare's London. One generation quickly forgets the prejudices of a previous one, but well into the twentieth century a genteel breeding and proper schooling were very important, especially within the highbrow culture of scholarship. Because Shakespeare's origins as the son of a Stratford trades-man had been carefully documented, he could not be given a new back-ground as Drayton was. The inescapable conclusion was drawn: someone more genteel had actually written Shakespeare's plays.

The standard biography of Drayton reflects the very same social preju-dices. No one in the seventeenth or eighteenth centuries thought that the sixteenth century had feudal households with "pages" and "minstrels." Elton speculated that Sir Henry Goodere had acted as Drayton's tutor. Elaborating upon this hint, the *DNB* article on Sir Henry Goodere the elder and his nephew, Sir Henry Goodere the younger, reports that Sir Henry the elder "is said to have helped Drayton at the university." No records exist to show that Drayton attended a university. Bernard Newdigate also surmises that after Drayton joined the Polesworth household he first shared a tutor with Frances Goodere (Newdigate, 18) and then acted as tutor to Sir Henry's younger daughter, Anne (Newdigate, 42). Samuel Daniel, who had a university degree, acted as a tutor as well as a secretary, but no specific evidence, even in Drayton's dedications, suggests that he acted as a tutor to wealthy and titled children. Even so, Newdigate describes him as the tutor of Frances and Anne Goodere; Lucy Harington Russell, Countess of Bedford; Elizabeth Tanfield, later Viscountess Falkland; and Sir Walter Aston (Newdigate, 42, 56, 78, 149).

Drayton and Anne Goodere   Perhaps because Drayton never married, Newdigate decided that his sonnet sequence, *Ideas Mirrour* (1594), revealed his passionate, lifelong devotion to Anne Goodere (42–44). Drayton's compliments to his patronesses are reinterpreted as allusions to Anne Goodere: "His devotion to Anne, recorded in poem after poem, in sea-son and out of season, does not weaken as he and she advance in years" (45). Even after Anne's marriage in 1595, as the story goes, Drayton remained faithful. He may have written a love lyric the night before he died. Newdigate describes this lyric as "a memorial of his devotion" to Anne

Goodere, from "the time when her 'eyes taught [him] the alphabet of love' down to the last day of his life" (223). Because of these romantic fabrications Drayton's early poems have not been treated as the bids for patronage that they clearly were. Kathleen Tillotson's notes are far more objective than Newdigate's biography (e.g., Tillotson, 214), but romantic flourishes have distorted our understanding of Drayton's clientage and social standing.

Servant to Thomas Goodere

Drayton was noticeably hostile to distinctions of class. In 1593 he described those who bragged of their lineage as "forgers of suppos'd Gentillitie" (1:65.18): "When he his great, great Grand-sires glory blases, / And paints out fictions in base coyned Phrases" (19–20). Drayton's numerous assaults on titles and privilege have been ignored because they do not ring true as the docile reflections of a "goodly page," but his documentary biography accounts for his resentment of class distinctions.

In 1598 Drayton was called by Margaret Saunders to act as a witness in a suit against the Gooderes over her jointure and her son's inheritance. The documents are complicated by the number of Henry Gooderes involved (for further clarification, see Appendix A, the Goodere genealogy). Sir Henry Goodere the elder (1534–95) had two brothers, William and Thomas, but no surviving male heirs. Both William and Thomas named their sons Henry Goodere after the owner of Polesworth. Sir Henry Goodere the elder, the knight who first owned Polesworth, needs to be distinguished from his nephew and son-in-law, Sir Henry Goodere the younger (1571–1627), who was the closest friend of John Donne. The other nephew, also a namesake, will be referred to as "Thomas' Henry." Sir Henry the elder was very fond of his brother Thomas; in 1574 or 1575 he settled his estate on Thomas, understanding that it would pass to his nephew, Thomas' Henry Goodere, but with the power of revocation. Thomas died in 1585, and in 1593 Sir Henry the elder resettled the Polesworth estate on his older daughter Frances after she had married his other nephew, William's son, Henry Goodere the younger.

Margaret Saunders later disputed the new settlement. When Thomas Goodere married her in 1573 or 1574, she was already the widow of a Nottinghamshire gentleman. Drayton would have been about ten years old at the time of the marriage. After his marriage, Thomas Goodere moved to his wife's estate at Collingham, Nottinghamshire; Thomas' Henry was born there in 1578, when Drayton was about fifteen.

A few days before Thomas died in 1585, according to Drayton's own testimony, Thomas told his wife Margaret to summon two servants "that be thy frendes that thou best lykest of," to act as witnesses to his statements about the disposition of the Collingham lease.[8] One of the two trusted servants whom Margaret selected was the twenty-two-year-old Michael Drayton. Since Thomas's statements about the Collingham lease concerned protection of Margaret's interests against encroachment by Thomas's brothers, William Goodere and Sir Henry Goodere of Polesworth, it is improbable that Margaret would have selected Michael Drayton as her witness had he grown up in the bosom of the Polesworth family.

Drayton testified on 16 August 1598, and is described as "xxxv. yeres or thereaboutes." His deposition, supported by other testimony, indicates that he had been a servant in the Collingham, Nottinghamshire, household for at least five years prior to Thomas's death. Drayton probably began his service when Margaret and Thomas were married in 1573, when he was about ten. Since Collingham, Nottinghamshire, was seventy miles distant from Polesworth, contact between the Collingham and Polesworth households cannot have been all that frequent.

No evidence exists that Drayton joined the Polesworth household after Thomas's death, but if we conjecture that he did, he was twenty-two or twenty-three years old, too old to act as a page or to share lessons with Frances Goodere. Although Drayton may have visited Polesworth, he did not grow up with Sir Henry's daughters. Moreover, his prefaces and dedications do not say that he did; the same social bias that conspired to confer gentility on the author of Shakespeare's plays furnished Drayton with an acceptable upbringing.

After confirming in his deposition that he was a servant in the home of Thomas Goodere and the now remarried Margaret Saunders, Drayton relates anecdotes, emphasizing the affection of Sir Henry the elder for Thomas's son, and he testifies that during the lifetime of Thomas, Thomas' Henry was regarded as the heir to Polesworth. His fidelity to the facts is not likely to have endeared Drayton to the new master of Polesworth, whose father was a defendant in the 1598 case. The second suit was brought in 1606 by Thomas' Henry, the son of Margaret and Thomas, against Sir Henry Goodere the younger. Drayton was not called as a witness in this second suit. The litigation was finally settled on 3 November 1606, but it had burdened the already impoverished estate. Polesworth was encumbered with debts because Sir Henry the elder, a Catholic who later conformed, had paid heavy fines and spent time in prison for his support of Mary Queen of Scots. Under James I Sir Henry the younger unsuccessfully tried to win reimbursement for the fines his uncle had incurred in support of James's mother. In 1599, the year following the court case, Henry Goodere the younger was in Ireland with Essex from whom he received his knighthood.

Drayton's background as a servant in the household of Thomas Goodere was respectable, but hardly genteel. To be a servant in the sixteenth century did not have the connotations that it appears to have had in the early twentieth century. It was not so much snobbery that Drayton faced, as it was the lack of social connections, the associations that a university background and membership in one of the Inns of Court supplied. John Donne had these credentials and a thorough understanding of the patronage system, gained while he served as secretary to Sir Thomas Egerton, Lord Keeper. Donne's connections and knowledge of the system made it possible for him to gain preferment even after he had jeopardized his position by marriage to an heiress without her father's consent. Lacking credentials, connections, and experience with the clientage system, Drayton faced extraordinary obstacles. Both his master, Thomas Goodere, and Sir Henry Goodere (1534–95) were dead before Drayton makes reference to the Gooderes. He appears to have hinted at a Polesworth connection to enhance his eligibility for literary clientage.

Early Clientage

Drayton had probably established himself in London by 1591. His *The Harmonie of the Church,* a series of verse translations of Old Testament prayers, was dedicated to Lady Jane Devereux, a landowner near his birthplace, Hartshill, in an epistle dated 10 February. A note in *Peirs Gaveston* mentions that Drayton has consulted John Stow's London library (1:208). Not one of Drayton's early poems is dedicated to the Gooderes. He dedicates *Idea The Shepheards Garland* (1593) to Robert Dudley, *Peirs Gaveston* (1593–94) to Henry Cavendish, and *Ideas Mirrour* (1594) to Anthony Cooke, all of whom had estates near Hartshill.

The Sidneys   Drayton's first efforts to win the patronage of prominent courtiers overlap his dedications to the gentry who had estates near Hartshill. He may have felt that it would be presumptuous to dedicate poetry to a prominent aristocrat without permission, and so he frequently worked his early appeals for patronage into the texts of his poems. His 1593 pastorals and 1594 sonnets aim at attracting the attention of the Countess of Pembroke, patroness of Edmund Spenser and Samuel Daniel. *Idea The Shepheards Garland* contains a pastoral elegy on Sir Philip Sidney, mourned as Elphin, god of poetry; this elegy is followed by a panegyric on Sidney's sister,

Mary Herbert, Countess of Pembroke, praised as Pandora, the true patroness of poetry.

His sonnet sequence, *Ideas Mirrour. Amours in Quatorzains* (1594), addresses Pandora, the name of the Countess of Pembroke in *Idea The Shepheards Garland*:

> Ankor triumph, upon whose blessed shore,
> The sacred Muses solemnize thy name:
> Where the *Arcadian* Swaines with rytes adore
> *Pandoras* poesy, and her living fame.
>
> (1:96.1–4)

He observes that his "thoughts, and fortunes all attend" this "myrror of *Ideas* praise" and concludes by identifying Mary as "the Queene of Poesie" (13, 18). This dedicatory sonnet is signed in italics, "Gorbo il fidele," an allusion to Gorbo, who praises the countess in *Idea The Shepheards Garland*.

Drayton concludes *Ideas Mirrour* with Amour 51, a testimonial to the Countess of Pembroke. In the second stanza he honors the learning of the countess and then offers an anagram for Mary Sidney:

> When you *Minerva* in the sunne behold,
> At her perfection stand you then and gaze,
> Where, in the compasse of a Marygold,
> *Meridianis* sits within a maze.
>
> (6–8)

"Meridianis," as Jean Robertson has pointed out, is an anagram for Mary Sidney.[9] The sonnet also includes allusions to Sidney's *Arcadia*. Dorus, an allusion to Prince Mucedorus in the *Arcadia,* is described as singing the love of his sweet Pamela while "Invention" vaunts the beauty of Minerva. This bid for patronage may not have been successful, but it illustrates Drayton's sense of literary and social hierarchy.

Lucy Harington   Drayton made his first overture to the wealthy Haringtons in the summer of 1594, shortly after he had published *Ideas Mirrour* (1594) with compliments to the Countess of Pembroke. He published *Matilda* (1594) with a fulsome dedication to Lucy Harington (1581–1627), alluding to the Goodere "Family" and the "House" of Polesworth, but not intimating that he had grown up at Polesworth with Sir Henry's daughters, Frances and Anne:

the exceeding kinde affection (which I knowe) the House of POWLESWORTH doe beare you, (a Family where-unto I must confesse, I am both in love and dutie more devote then to any other) hath mooved mee, for a more particuler proofe of that honor which both they and I are willing to doe you, to dedicate my Poeme to your protection. (1:210)

He asks Lucy "graciously to patronize" *Matilda* and alludes to the "House of POWLESWORTH" in order to make the most of the Gooderes' connections to the Harington family. His dedication was exceedingly well timed for that purpose. Sir Henry Goodere the younger, heir to Polesworth, had married his cousin Frances in 1593; their daughter was born in 1594, the year that *Matilda* appeared. She was named Lucy in honor of her godmother, Lucy Harington, who later generously subsidized her marriage to Sir Francis Nethersole.[10]

In 1595 Drayton dedicated *Endimion and Phoebe* to Lucy, after her marriage to Edward Russell, Earl of Bedford, promising that he would undertake no subject other than the countess, "upon whose prayse my soule shall spend her powers" (1:126.12). Lucy means *light,* and Drayton's portrait of Phoebe, goddess of the moon, compliments her. The two commendatory poems by E.P. and S.G. praise "Idea," the mistress-muse of Drayton's pastoral and sonnets, suggesting that Lucy represented "Idea," at least in 1594.

In 1596, the following year, Drayton published *Mortimeriados,* his first attempt at epic, and his latest versions of *Peirs Gaveston* and *Matilda* as well as his new complaint, *Robert of Normandy.* These poems again appeared with effusive dedications to Lucy. The dedication to *Mortimeriados* is especially laudatory, praising the Haringtons, Lucy's family by birth, and the Bedfords, her family by marriage, and acknowledging her kinship with the Sidneys. Drayton concludes by promising that her name "shall lyve in steele-out-during rimes" (1:307.45), but he has not yet mastered the rhetoric of clientage. He informs his patroness that his verse will endow her with more credit than "earthly honors" or a "Countesse name" (1:307.57).[11] After promising that Lucy will live forever in the "immortall toombe" (59) of his poem, he addresses her as "my hope, my Lady, and my Muse," epithets that indicate Lucy continues to embody "Idea" in 1596 (63).

Englands Heroicall Epistles Drayton's *Englands Heroicall Epistles* (1597), a more emphatic bid for patronage, appeared with nine dedications. Although the Bedfords are still central figures, Drayton now casts his net more widely. For the first time in his career he stresses his connection with the Gooderes. In the dedication addressed to Lucy's husband, the Earl of

Bedford, he claims that Sir Henry Goodere the elder "bequeathed" him to the service of Lucy Harington, now the Countess of Bedford, before his death in 1595:

> to whose service I was first bequeathed, by that learned and accomplished Gentleman, *Sir Henry Goodere* (not long since deceased,) whose I was whilst he was: whose patience pleased to beare with the imperfections of my heedlesse and unstaied youth. That excellent and matchlesse Gentleman, was the first cherisher of my Muse, which had been by his death left a poore Orphane to the worlde, had hee not before bequeathed it to that Lady whom he so deerly loved. (Tillotson, 112)

If the owner of Polesworth were going to bequeath Drayton to anyone before his death in 1595, he presumably would have bequeathed him to his heir and older daughter Frances, or to his younger daughter Anne, not to his thirteen-year-old neighbor Lucy Harington! Drayton's suggestion that without Lucy's support his muse would have been "left a poor Orphane to the worlde," if interpreted literally, would mean that Sir Henry the younger (1571–1627) had no interest in Drayton. If this 1597 dedication is compared with earlier prefaces addressed to Lucy, discrepancies in fact and tone confirm that Drayton was simply putting the best possible face on his Goodere connection. He also dedicates poems to Sir Henry the younger and to Frances Goodere, thanking the Goodere family "for the most part of [his] education" (Tillotson, 129) and claiming lifelong acquaintanceship with Frances's "milde disposition" (134). He mentions neither Anne Goodere, who had married Sir Henry Rainsford after her father's death, nor her husband, but Lucy's mother, Anne Harington, receives a warm dedication.

The sequence of Drayton's dedications makes sense only if we assume that he was not intimately acquainted with any of these people, but hoped to consolidate his position as Lucy's client and continue her "sweet golden showers" (1:126.10). After several years of publishing poems, Drayton alluded to the "Goodere family" and "Polesworth household" to embellish his service in Thomas Goodere's household. For the same reason, he credits the Gooderes with his education.

When *Englands Heroicall Epistles* appeared in 1597, it was an immediate and astonishing success, rapidly going through more editions in the same time period than Spenser's *Faerie Queene*. But as an appeal for patronage, it may well have been a disaster. Drayton sought recognition from the elite and powerful, from the audience to whom Spenser had appealed, but his *Englands Heroicall Epistles* was not veiled with the "dark conceit" of Spenser's *Faerie Queene*. His historical message was plain.

Drayton concluded *Englands Heroicall Epistles* with epistles exchanged, first, between Mary Tudor, sister of Henry VIII, and wife to Charles Brandon, Duke of Suffolk; and second, between Lady Jane Grey and Guilford Dudley. Drayton's audience was well aware that these were the ancestors of Viscount Beauchamp, the son of Catherine Grey and Edward Seymour, Earl of Hertford, and a major claimant to the English throne. In the late 1590s the succession question eclipsed all other issues in importance: political concern was heightened by Elizabeth's advanced age and by the number of potential claimants. In 1597, the year that *Englands Heroicall Epistles* appeared, James of Scotland had increased tension by asking to be created Prince of Wales and identified as Elizabeth's successor.

Drayton included dedications to two Catholic noblemen in the 1597 edition, but both of these dedications were removed from the 1598 edition. These particular dedicatees would not have wanted to be associated with a poem that appeared to oppose James's succession. The Catholic William Parker, fourth Baron Monteagle, belonged to the Essex faction that supported James. He later suffered heavy fines and imprisonment for his participation in the Essex rebellion. The other dedicatee, the learned Lord Henry Howard, the second son of the poet Henry Howard, Earl of Surrey, was a disaffected Catholic already in close contact with James.

If Michael Drayton had merely withdrawn the Monteagle and Howard dedications, we might assume that they were removed because patronage was not forthcoming. However, in 1598 and 1599, along with new epistles designed to make the poem less susceptible to political interpretation, Drayton added two new dedications that comment upon patronage in an aggrieved tone. Since the dedications to Monteagle and Howard were removed before the second edition in 1598, these two noblemen probably snubbed Drayton or insisted that he remove references to them from his poem. In the new 1598 dedication, addressed to Mr. Henry Lucas, son to Edward Lucas, Esq., Drayton complains that he has been the victim of ingratitude: "Many there be in England, of whome for some particularity I might justly challenge greater merit, had I not beene borne in so evill an howre, as to be poisoned with that gaule of ingratitude" (Tillotson, 132). Since *Englands Heroicall Epistles* was extremely popular, his reference to the "gaule of ingratitude" must refer to the failure of his efforts at patronage.

His 1599 dedication to Maister James Huish, an untitled commoner without the status of Esquire, takes a dim view of noble patronage. Drayton begins with a history of the custom of using dedications:

It is seated by custome . . . to beare the names of our friends upon the fronts of our bookes, as Gentlemen use to set theyr Armes over theyr gates. Some say this use beganne by the Heroes and brave spirits of the old world, which were desirous to bee thought to patronize learning; and men in requitall honour the names of those brave Princes. (Tillotson, 121)

Drayton's 1597 dedication to Lord Henry Howard addressed him specifically as a learned man whose approbation Drayton sought on the grounds of Howard's knowledge (Tillotson, 117), but here he insinuates that Lord Henry Howard is not one of those "brave Princes" willing to patronize learning. Significantly, Drayton disclaims any interest in the patronage of "great men": "But for mine owne part (not to dissemble) I find no such vertue in any of their great titles to doe so much for any thing of mine, and so let them passe" (Tillotson, 121). Abandoning the humble stance of the client, Drayton defiantly insists that he finds no "vertue in any of their great titles to doe so much for any thing of mine." His needless assertion underscores his resentment of rank and privilege.

Although eager to win recognition from a courtly audience, Drayton lacked the diplomatic understanding of the elite that came naturally to men such as Ben Jonson.[12] He also lacked a judicious understanding of the political scene. He cannot have been ignorant of the political thrust of *Englands Heroicall Epistles,* but he severely underestimated the volatility of the contemporary situation. The breach between Essex and Elizabeth was widening, and Essex's supporters were trying to forge a faction made up of Catholics and left-wing Puritans.

To make *Englands Heroicall Epistles* less susceptible to political interpretation, Drayton added to and revised the poem in 1598, 1599, and 1600. The implications of these changes for the interpretation of *Englands Heroicall Epistles* will be discussed in chapter 3. But these politic revisions did not redeem Drayton. His image was controversial. A prominent courtier would not have regarded Drayton as a safe client whose circumspect behavior could be taken for granted.

The Theater   In 1598 Drayton began to write for the professional theater. His success in handling English history in *Englands Heroicall Epistles* may have made him attractive to the Admiral's Men as a collaborator on chronicle plays. In the eighth eclogue (1–20) of *Idea The Shepheards Garland* (1593), Drayton denigrates those who write for the stage, but the many lines that he later echoes from Marlowe and Shakespeare indicate that their plays changed his mind.

The Admiral's Men was officially under the sponsorship of Thomas Howard of Effingham, Lord High Admiral of England. Edward Alleyn, the principal shareholder and actor of the company, had married the stepdaughter of Philip Henslowe, who owned both the Rose and Fortune theaters. From *Henslowe's Diary,* a book of receipts and records of payments, as well as from other contemporary sources, we can reconstruct Drayton's dramatic career. He and his collaborators wrote thirteen plays in the summer season of 1598, two in 1599, three in 1600, and one each in 1601 and 1602.[13] Drayton may also have collaborated on *The London Prodigal* sometime between 1603 and 1605. He rarely wrote a play by himself (see Appendix B for a list of his plays, including collaborators and likely dates). Of his twenty or twenty-one plays, only *I Sir John Oldcastle* was printed and has survived.[14] In 1598, while Drayton was writing for the public theater, he appeared as a witness for the much-married and much-widowed Margaret Saunders in her lawsuit against William Goodere, father of the heir to Polesworth.

Englands Heroicall Epistles   In 1600, after Sir John Hayward was imprisoned for publishing a history about the deposition of Richard II by Henry IV, Drayton revised his epistles of Richard II. He also included the latest versions of his sonnets with *Englands Heroicall Epistles* and pointedly added a sonnet addressed to King James of Scotland. Drayton was belatedly endorsing James's claim and disclaiming the support for the Suffolk claimant implied in *Englands Heroicall Epistles* (1597). To address a sonnet to James in 1600 was daring even for a poet who had decided not to depend on the "great titles" of the elite. Drayton stressed James's poetic talents, but the timing of his sonnet, to say the least, was premature. Elizabeth, the reigning monarch, had not yet named a successor.

The Patronage of Sir Walter Aston   In the 1602 edition of *Englands Heroicall Epistles* Drayton dedicated the undedicated epistles of Edward the Black Prince and Alice, Countess of Salisbury, to Sir Walter Aston (1583–1639). Drayton may have become acquainted with Aston while still in Warwickshire.[15] Sir Walter Aston's mother was the daughter of Sir Thomas Lucy, and Aston and his sisters were brought up at Charlecote, the Lucy estate; through the Lucys, Aston was also a first cousin of Sir Henry Rainsford, who married Anne Goodere.

Aston was a very wealthy man with estates in Stafford, Derby, Leicester, and Warwick counties and rents reputed to exceed ten thousand pounds a year. This patronage relationship may not have been based on Drayton's poetry. Drayton wrote no entertainments for the Aston family and only one polite verse epistle to Aston's wife. Since Aston was less than twenty years old when he became Drayton's patron, he may not have minded Drayton's reputation for indiscretion and may have hired him as a secretary because he valued his learning.[16] When Sir Walter was created a Knight of the Bath at James's coronation, Drayton acted as his esquire.

Royal Patronage

Drayton never wrote for the Jacobean court and addressed no verse to James after 20 March 1604. In *Poly-Olbion* (1613) he blames his delay in completing the poem on lack of royal support: "finding the times since his Majesties happy coming in, to fall so heavily upon my distressed fortunes, . . . But I instantly saw all my long nourisht hopes even buried alive before my face" (4:vi).

Drayton's editors unequivocally ascribe his isolation from the court to a social miscalculation. He is described as naively violating decorum by failing to mourn Elizabeth I in his 1603 welcoming poem, "To the Majestie of King James" (Newdigate, 124–27; Tillotson, 53–55). Without even a trace of qualification, Tillotson comments:

No poet save Drayton omits all reference to the late Queen. His silence on the subject, in a poem issued while she was still unburied, must have seemed not merely an outrageous error of taste, but a serious false step for one seeking royal favour. . . . It is indeed ironical that the one occasion when Drayton was ahead of fashion should have nearly ruined his career as a poet and left a bitterness which lasted the rest of his life." (Tillotson, 53, 54)

This same explanation for Drayton's isolation from the court is repeated by every scholar who discusses Drayton's fortunes under James.[17]

Drayton was prevented from gaining the recognition he wanted by what he regarded as his integrity, but what a more astute politician would have called brash presumption. The myth of his "outrageous error of taste" in failing to mourn Elizabeth needs to be put to rest along with the myths of his genteel upbringing and lifelong devotion to Anne Goodere. In 1603 those courtiers who did not set out immediately for Scotland were carefully planning their entertainments for the new king's progress south.

Drayton's editors offer two pieces of evidence for their hypothesis: first, Drayton's internal allusion to his "forward pen" in his elegy to "Mr. George Sandys" (1627), and second, a contemporary reference by Henry Chettle to Drayton's having praised the new king before he mourned the late queen.

The Sandys's reference was written over twenty years after James's succession and published two years after James's death; further, the language is ambiguous and may refer to a poem written before 1603:

> It was my hap before all other men
> To suffer shipwrack by my forward pen:
> When King James entred; at which joyfull time
> I taught his title to this Ile in rime
>
> (3:206.19–22)

In addition to meaning "premature," Drayton's phrase "forward pen" also has the connotations of "forward" as opposed to "froward." Spenser, for example, uses "forward" to mean aggressive in book 2 of *The Faerie Queene.* Even if the meaning "premature" for "forward" is insisted upon, Drayton's allusion to his "forward pen" probably refers to his sonnet to James in 1600. Since Drayton also claims to have been the first poet to address James, this sonnet corresponds with that chronology.

The second piece of evidence is cited from a poem by Henry Chettle. Chettle, one of Drayton's collaborators when working for the Admiral's Men, entered *Englandes Mourning Garment* in the Stationers' Register on 25 April 1603. His poem was rushed to the printers to reveal the processional order of Elizabeth's funeral before it took place on 28 April. In a similar incident involving Henry Petowe, the printer was fined for revealing the funeral ceremony before it had occurred.[18] Since the timing of Elizabeth's death could not be foreseen, if Drayton worked as rapidly as Chettle, then his "To His Majestie" (not entered in the Stationers' Register) may have appeared just before *Englandes Mourning Garment*, a few days before Elizabeth's funeral on 28 April.

In *Englandes Mourning Garment* Chettle asserts that kings should never be criticized; God alone should correct royal faults. Then he offers advice in a strangely disjointed series of anti-Spanish and anti-Irish diatribes, the latter including a tribute to Elizabeth I for not endorsing the poisoning of Irish rebels. Chettle also censures a number of contemporary poets for not mourning the queen. Drayton is by no means singled out. Chettle chides his contemporaries in the following order: Samuel Daniel, William Warner, George Chapman, Ben Jonson, William Shakespeare, Michael Drayton, Thomas Lodge, Thomas Dekker, John Marston, and Henry Petowe.

A more complete excerpt of the poem than is usually given supplies the essential context for the criticism of Drayton:

> Nor doth one Poet seeke her name to raise,
> That Living, hourely striu'd to sing her praise.
> He that so well could sing the fatall strife
> Betweene the royall Roses White and Red
> That prais'd so oft Eliza in her life,
> His Muse seemes now to dye, as shee is dead.
>> Thou sweetest song-man of all English swaines,
>> Awake for shame, honour ensues thy paines.[19]

Samuel Daniel is told to "awake for shame," and then Shakespeare is depicted as ungrateful:

> Nor doth the silver tonged *Melicert,*
> Drop from his honied muse one sable teare
> To mourne her death that graced his desert,
> And to his laies opend her Royall eare.
>> Shepheard, remember our *Elizabeth,*
>> And sing her rape, done by that *Tarquin,* Death.
>> (72)

Drayton is treated more kindly than Daniel or Shakespeare because Chettle acknowledges that Drayton loved Elizabeth:

> No lesse doe thou (sweete singer *Coridon*);
> The Theame exceedeth *Edwards Isabell,*
> Forget her not in *Poly-Albion;*
> Make some amends, I know thou lovdst her well.
>> Thinke twas a fault to haue thy Verses seene
>> Praising the king, ere they had mournd the Queen.
>> (73)

To his contemporaries, Chettle hardly represented the voice of decorum. *Englandes Mourning Garment* was repeatedly satirized as an offensive attempt to make money out of the queen's death.[20]

In any case, in 1603, moving eulogies to Elizabeth did not insure preferment in the Jacobean court. Drayton had already jeopardized his fortunes with James by his tribute to the Suffolk claimant in *Englands Heroicall Epistles.* The chronological record of James's progress into England demonstrates that Drayton was not included in any of the many private festivities hosted by powerful courtiers. On 23 April 1603 Samuel Daniel's *A Panegyrike congratulatorie to the kings majestie* was presented to King James under the auspices of Lucy, Countess of Bedford, when James was entertained at the Harington family estate. The title page to *A Panegyrike congratulatorie* states that Daniel personally delivered the poem to James. A few months later Lucy arranged for Daniel to present his *Vision of the Twelve Goddesses* at Hampton Court on 8 January 1( )4. She also promoted Ben Jonson's efforts to gain recognition by the court.[21] It must have been especially galling to Drayton that Lucy, whose patronage he had enjoyed, was achieving such prominence in the new court while ignoring him entirely.

Although Drayton's editors claim that he wrote the only poem that welcomed James without mourning Elizabeth, Ben Jonson does not mourn Elizabeth in the entertainment that he wrote for presentation on 25 June 1603 at Althorp, the seat of Sir Robert Spencer. But Jonson does remark, in greeting Queen Anne, "Long live Oriana / T'exceed, whom she succeeds, our late Diana."[22] Probably as a means of safely instructing the new monarch, Jonson satirically describes the court of Elizabeth I as one requiring bribes, pliant smiles, and flattery, but assumes that the new regime will be more responsive to virtue. Jonson did not just praise the new queen without mourning the old; he flattered Anne by disparaging Elizabeth.

Emphasis on the timing of Drayton's "To his Majestie" has taken attention away from the text. If James read this poem, a speculation in itself, he might well be offended by Drayton's stern advice that he must banish from his court "the foole, the Pandar, and the Parasite" (1:475.168):

> The very earthl'est & degenerat'st spirit,
> That is most voyd of vertue, and of merit,
> With the austeer'st, and impudentest face,
> Will thrust himselfe the formost to thy grace;
> Those silken, laced, and perfumed hinds,
> That have rich bodies, but poore wretched minds
> (161–66)

Drayton's willingness to instruct the new king on how to organize his court may not have favorably impressed James. But "To his Majestie" could only be described as warmly ingratiating if compared with *The Owle,* the biting satire that Drayton entered in the Stationers' Register on 8 February 1604, just prior to the triumphal entrance of the royal family into London on 15 March. His public offering for the entry, "A Paean Triumphall" (1604), praises the royal family, but concentrates on a history of the goldsmith's guild who sponsored the poem. The first editions of "To his Majestie" (1603) and "A Paean

Triumphall" (1604) were also the last. Drayton never reprinted either of these tributes to James in later collections of his poetry.

Lucy, Countess of Bedford   Drayton realized that he had little chance of regaining Lucy's favor by 1604, when Daniel and Jonson became favored literary figures at court, but he cannot have foreseen how powerful the countess would, in fact, become. Her father, Sir John Harington of Exton, and her mother, the heiress Anne Kelway, were made the guardians of James's daughter, Princess Elizabeth. The Countess of Bedford became a favorite of Queen Anne's, a performer in court masques, and an influential power broker in the competition for preferment. Her beauty, wit, and virtue were celebrated by Samuel Daniel, Ben Jonson, and John Donne.

As Drayton gradually realized the extent of Lucy's influence, he also recognized that he was going to be ignored by the very audience he valued most, the audience to whom Edmund Spenser had appealed. But he still had choices. He could have overcome his reputation for indiscretion by using the complex network of court patronage to regain favor. He could have abased himself to Lucy, Countess of Bedford, or begged assistance from Sir Henry Goodere, who was her client. He could have tried to ingratiate himself with James's favorites, as Donne managed, but Drayton offered no accommodation.

Once he understood that his laureate ambitions would be ignored by the court, Drayton launched a breathtaking attack on Lucy, Countess of Bedford, who, after the queen, had become the court's most prominent female figure. In 1606 he reprinted *Idea The Shepheards Garland* (1593) as *Poemes lyrick and pastorall* with a new version of the eighth eclogue. In it he portrays Lucy as Selena, a faithless patroness who has deserted the faithful Rowland to favor Cerberon, a "beastly clowne," figuratively named after the three-headed dog who guards the gates to hell.

In the concluding lines of his invective Drayton consigns Lucy's name to oblivion, taking back his earlier dedications that promised her immortality:

> Let age sit soone and ugly on her brow,
> No sheepheards praises living let her have
> To her last end noe creature pay one vow
> Nor flower be strew'd on her forgotten grave,
> And to the last of all devouring tyme
> Nere be her name remembred more in rime.
>   (Tillotson, 189.103–8)

He calls for "age" to make this reigning beauty old and ugly before her time: "Let age sit soone and ugly on her brow." His curse condemns Lucy to unhappiness while she lives and oblivion after she dies. In 1619, when he prepared a folio collection of his early work, he removed the passages attacking Selena, but he also eliminated all dedications and complimentary poems addressed to Lucy during the 1590s.[23]

1607–1619   On 12 August 1607 Drayton joined a group that hoped to establish a company called Children of the King's Revels at Whitefriars. He was associated with Lordinge Barry, William Treville, William Cooke, Edward Sibthorpe, and John Mason, all of whom became bound "jointly and severally" to Thomas Woodforde for the sum of one hundred twenty pounds (Newdigate, 112–23). The Children of the Queen's Revels, for whom Samuel Daniel acted as licenser, had received royal protection under patent in 1604, and this company hoped to achieve a similar success. The Children of the King's Revels failed miserably; by 1609 Whitefriars was in the possession of the Children of the Queen's Revels, but a series of court cases concerning the Children of the King's Revels continued well into the seventeenth century.[24]

Poly-Olbion   In 1612 the first part of *Poly-Olbion* appeared with a dedication to Prince Henry, the royal symbol of Elizabethan values. Drayton's bid for favor was successful, but fate interfered because Prince Henry, heir to the throne, died on 6 November 1612. Henry's household accounts record grants of pensions of twenty pounds to Joshua Sylvester and ten pounds to Michael Drayton (Newdigate, 160). Although Drayton received a pension from Prince Henry, the first part of *Poly-Olbion* was not a popular success. The second part of *Poly-Olbion* was completed in 1618, but Drayton was not able to find a printer until 1622. While attempting to find a printer and bookseller, Drayton began a correspondence in 1618 with the Scottish poet, William Drummond of Hawthornden. He probably wrote to Drummond at the suggestion of their mutual Scottish friend, Sir William Alexander; he asked Drummond to put him in touch with Andro Hart, the Edinburgh bookseller, who had published Drummond's work. Although the two men never met, they corresponded intermittently until Drayton's death in 1631.[25] After Drayton's death Drummond expressed interest in bringing out any manuscripts of *Poly-Olbion* that survived and eloquently prophesied that its author would "live by all likelihood so long as . . . men speak English" (Newdigate, 189).

1619 Folio The 1619 folio contains the final versions of Drayton's early poems and is dedicated to Sir Walter Aston. Aston's patronage of Drayton ended in 1619, if not before. In 1619 King James appointed Sir Walter ambassador to Spain, charging him with negotiation of a Spanish Catholic marriage for Prince Charles. Drayton's elegies explicitly criticize James's pro-Spanish foreign policy (3:206–12, 238–41), but they were not published until after James's death in 1625. Drayton revised his 1606 odes, adding a new dedication to "My Noble Friend, Sir Henry Goodere, a Gentleman of His Majesties Privie Chamber" (2:344). This 1619 dedication is the first reference to Sir Henry Goodere since Drayton's deposition in the 1598 court case. Goodere's wife and sister-in-law, Frances and Anne Goodere, respectively, were praised in the pastorals of 1606, but Sir Henry was not mentioned. Drayton's dedication cannot have been motivated by expectations of patronage. Sir Henry Goodere (1571–1627) was deeply in debt; his estate was settled on trustees. Michael Drayton, perhaps under Aston's auspices, acted as one of the sureties in this 1618 settlement.[26] In spite of futile letters and poems of praise to Buckingham, Goodere was finally reduced to existing from year to year on warrants that protected him from arrest.

When Sir Henry Rainsford, kinsman of Aston and husband of Anne Goodere, died on 27 January 1622, Drayton wrote an elegy, "Upon the Death of his Incomparable Friend, Sir Henry Raynsford of Clifford." This elegy uses the death of Sir Henry as an emblem of human mortality and movingly describes him as "so fast a friend, so true a Patriot" (3:234.104). Sir Henry's widow, Anne Goodere Rainsford, is not mentioned in the funeral elegy.

1627 and 1630 Folios After the appearance of *Poly-Olbion* (1622) Drayton published two more collections of poetry. The collection entitled *The Battaile of Agincourt* (1627) was comprehensively dedicated to those noble men who had the magnanimity of their courageous ancestors and who respected poetry. Drayton addressed copies with more specific dedications to potential patrons.

His last folio collection appeared in 1630 under the title of one of his finest poems: *The Muses Elizium*. This volume also contained two new divine poems, *Noahs Flood* and *David and Goliah,* and reprinted a poem published in 1604 under the new title, *Moses His Birth and Miracles*. This collection was dedicated to Edward Sackville, fourth Earl of Dorset, the grandson of Thomas Sackville, first Earl of Dorset, author of the "Induction" to *A Mirror for Magistrates* (1563). In his dedication Drayton says that the constancy of

Sackville's favors since they first began "have now made me one of your family, and I am become happy in the title to be called Yours" (3:246). This heightened rhetoric should not be interpreted literally, as it has been. There is no evidence that Drayton received any more patronage from Dorset than did a number of other poets: Donne was his guest at Knole; Jonson praised his liberality; Robert Herrick approved of his talents as a literary critic. Without documentary evidence we should not assume that Drayton found "a second golden age in the protection of the house of Dorset" (Tillotson, 220; Newdigate, 211–14).

Michael Drayton was buried in Westminster Abbey in 1631, under the north wall. A statue was erected for him in the poet's corner near Geoffrey Chaucer and William Shakespeare, an indication of the high esteem in which he was held when he died. On the monument, the following inscription was placed:

> Doe pious Marble: Let thy Readers Knowe
> What they, and what their children owe
> To *Draitons* Name. (Newdigate, 220)

This noble tribute expressing the conviction that Drayton's name "cannot fade" should be juxtaposed to Henry Peacham's comments on Drayton's lack of worldly success: "Honest Mr. *Michael Drayton* had about some five pounds lying by him at his death."[27] In the final inventory of his goods his brother Edmund reported his estate at £24 8s. 2d. (Newdigate, 222).

Another measure of success probably meant more to Michael Drayton. For Drayton's 1627 folio Ben Jonson wrote "The Vision of Ben. Jonson, On the Muses of His Friend, M. Drayton." Jonson extends a noble tribute to a man who, like himself, followed the muse throughout his long life. Jonson's poem is especially moving because he praises his fellow poet in images that Drayton himself might have chosen:

> I saw a Beauty from the Sea to rise,
> That all Earth look'd on; and that earth, all Eyes!
> It cast a beame as when the chear-full Sun.
> Is fayre got up, and day some houres begun!
>   (3:3.15–18)

From the image of a "chear-full Sun . . . fayre got up," Jonson uncharacteristically moves to the numerology of heaven, honoring Drayton by echoing the kind of allusion he had used so exuberantly in his early verse:

This engraving of "Ruins of Tixall" is reproduced from Arthur Clifford's *Tixall Poetry* (London, 1813) with the permission of the Henry E. Huntington Library, San Marino, California.

That Orbe was cut forth into Regions seaven.
And those so sweet, and well proportion'd parts,
As it had beene the circle of the Arts!
When by thy bright *Ideas* standing by,
I found it pure, and perfect *Poesy.*

(20–25)

Drayton did not fulfill his laureate ambitions, but he received a poetic accolade, a symbolic laurel, from Ben Jonson, the most successful and respected literary figure of his generation.

Chapter Two
Apprenticeship: 1591–1597

Drayton's first published work, *The Harmonie of the Church,* verse translations from Old Testament prayers, appeared in 1591, followed two years
later by his more ambitious pastoral eclogues.[1] Between 1591 and 1597,
when *Englands Heroicall Epistles* appeared, Drayton experimented with a series of related genres, including the pastoral, the sonnet sequence, and the
minor epic. His efforts in these genres were related, as repetition of "Idea" in
the title of each poem suggests: *Idea The Shepheards Garland* (1593), *Ideas
Mirrour* (1594), *Endimion and Phoebe. Ideas Latmus* (1595). In these poems
Drayton explores the "Idea" of poetry, but he is especially concerned with its
aesthetic principles. He also dedicates each of his early poems to a specific patron from whom he hopes to receive patronage, but in *Idea The Shepheards
Garland,* his first secular poem, he also raises the larger issue of how patronage affects poetics.

Drayton belongs to the group of "self-crowned laureates" whom Richard
Helgerson has identified as consciously shaping their careers in imitation of
Vergil and as aspiring to laureate status.[2] Using Vergil's literary career as a
model, the aspiring poet was to begin with a pastoral modeled on Vergil's *Eclogues;* followed by a minor epic, or a work imitating the *Georgics;* and then
crown his achievements with the epic. Edmund Spenser, only a decade older
than Drayton, had followed this schedule, moving from *The Shepheardes
Calender* (1579) to *The Faerie Queene* (1590). Drayton intended *Idea The
Shepheards Garland* as a laureate gesture that would signal his aspiration.

Laureateship, however, required that a poet's stature be acknowledged.
Recognition as a laureate conferred both social and literary status. Sir Philip
Sidney's *Astrophil and Stella* (1591) had appeared six years after his heroic
death in the Netherlands; his *Defence of Poesy,* which circulated widely in
manuscript, was to appear in print in 1595. Drayton describes Sidney's sister,
Mary Herbert, Countess of Pembroke, as the "Queen of Poesie." Although
Idea The Shepheards Garland is dedicated to Robert Dudley, whose estate
was near Hartshill, within the text of the poem Drayton solicits the literary
recognition of Sidney's sister.

The Pastoral: *Idea The Shepheards Garland*

Drayton carefully organized the nine pastoral eclogues in *Idea The Shepheards Garland* as a poetic manifesto. The pastoral offered him an opportunity to experiment with a number of verse forms, such as debate, elegy, and eulogy, as well as a number of metric patterns. His structure borrows from Vergil's *Eclogues*. Vergil uses his fifth eclogue, a pastoral elegy for Daphnis, as a vehicle to present the apotheosis of Julius Caesar.[3] In his fifth eclogue Drayton offers an apotheosis of the "Idea" of poetry, but he departs from his Vergilian model by including nine rather than ten eclogues. He does so because he wants to achieve the effect explained by his subtitle, *Idea The Shepheards Garland: Rowlands Sacrifice to the Nine Muses*. His nine eclogues form a garland that will crown Drayton's "Idea" of poetry, while honoring the nine Muses who preside over learning.

To suggest this circular structure, he pairs the first four eclogues with the last four so that, like a garland, they surround the apotheosis of poetry in the fifth. Within the garland structure, the first and ninth eclogues present laments by Rowland, functioning as Drayton's persona (as Colin Clout does for Spenser). In the first eclogue the joyful spring is contrasted with Rowland's contrition for his follies, but his unhappy thoughts are swept away by poetic inspiration. He cries out "like one surprisde with sodaine lunacie" (76).[4] Carried away with ecstasy, he exclaims: "Flye whirle-winde thoughts unto the heavens" (78). Rowland's inspiration establishes the theme of "poetry as an Idea" that Drayton intends to serve as the thematic link among the nine eclogues.

Drayton only partially succeeds in unifying his 1593 pastorals. No relationship is established between the poet's "sodaine lunacie" and the despair and suffering of the Petrarchan lover, a theme in the second, seventh, and ninth eclogues. In the second eclogue the youthful Motto is warned by the fatherly Winken that love brings woe and pain. In the seventh the elderly Borrill tries to convince the youthful Batte that love is dangerous, but Batte, unlike Motto, refuses to listen to the older shepherd's advice. These dialogues about love foreshadow the melancholy resolution of the ninth eclogue, which dwells on Rowland's unrequited love for Idea.

The fourth, fifth, and sixth eclogues function as the poetic core of *Idea The Shepheards Garland*. The fourth eclogue, a pastoral elegy, laments the death of Elphin, Sir Philip Sidney. Drayton celebrates Sidney as "the Immortall mirror of all Poesie" (110). His death has deprived poetry of its best spokesman and main support. The fifth eclogue begins with a dialogue in which Motto and Rowland discuss contemporary abuses of poetry. Drayton devotes the first sixty lines, nearly one-third of the fifth eclogue, to a scathing analysis of how literary clientage affects poetry. This dialogue is followed by the apotheosis of Idea that functions as Drayton's poetic manifesto.

Any poet who could name his muse "Idea" would have to be a Platonist, and Drayton does not disappoint us. He begins the fifth eclogue with a brief explanation of how poets come into being. As we would expect, poets are born, not made; nature has bequeathed to them talents "[t]hat mighty Monarchs seldome have possest" (12). Heaven inspires them with a "most divine impression" (14). All of this is quite conventional, but it leads Drayton to a highly unconventional attack on those who pride themselves on rank and lineage. These "forgers of suppos'd Gentillitie" (18) derive their coats of arms from their ancestors' achievements: "When he his great, great Grand-sires glory blases, / And paints out fictions in base coyned Phrases" (19–20). Drayton's inadequate social credentials, his conscious-ness of his own social vulnerability may explain his criticism. His resent-ment of class distinctions may have prompted him to remark that "[t]rue valeur lodgeth in the lowliest harts" (28) but, less conventionally, he adds, "vertue is in the minde, not in th'attyre" (29). Sixteenth-century sumptu-ary laws regulated dress according to class; dismissal of this symbol of social distinctions might make a courtier uneasy.

After juxtaposing the superficiality of rank and class with the worthiness of talent and virtue, Drayton turns to poets who, because they belong to a corrupt society, prostitute their talents. After dooming to "eternal death" (50) those poets who slander to gain a reputation, he unleashes his scorn on those ambitious poets who use the style of "Worlds fawning fraud" (38) to curry favor with the powerful. He vows that his poetry will be "free from ser-vile thrall" (45):

> Nor caps, nor curtsies to a paynted wall,
> Nor heaping rotten sticks on needles fires,
> Ambitious thoughts to clime nor feares to fall.
> (42–44)

The vivid image of accommodating literary clients as making "curtsies to a paynted wall" underlines his passionate insistence on his integrity. This au-tonomy, of course, compliments the virtue of those from whom Drayton so-licits patronage. His patrons will understand that poetry and virtue are inseparable, that flattery depreciates the recipient. Even so, Drayton's fiercely evocative image of courtly compliment as "heaping rotten sticks on needles fires" reveals his deep resentment of the client's "servile thrall" (45).

After analyzing the social misuse of poetry, Drayton offers a *blazon* of Idea, his concept of poetry. Although there are hints of Idea's physical charms (78–101), she rapidly becomes the virtuous light that illuminates her context. She becomes "That cleare which doth worlds cleernes quite surpasse" (102–3). Joan Grundy has convincingly demonstrated that "clear" had a complex meaning for Drayton, representing "something knowledgeable, visionary, heroic in theme and spirit, perspicuous, and shiningly beautiful."[5] Grundy does not include *Idea The Shepheards Garland* in her discussion, but it is significant that "Idea" epitomizes and transcends "[t]hat cleare which doth worlds cleerenes quite surpasse" (103).

Embodying the beauty of nature, poetry is "Mornings vermilion, verdant spring-times pride" (108). Poetry also becomes the primal source of all art and learning:

> That stately Theater on whose fayre stage,
> Each morall vertue actes a princely part,
> Where every scene pronounced by a Sage,
> Eternizeth divinest Poets Arte.
> (117–20)

The diction in this passage emphasizes the social function of poetry and its political importance. Poetry is the "stately Theater" upon which virtue plays a "princely part." Poetry's wisdom insures that the scenes played in England's "stately Theater" will be "pronounced by a Sage" and given immortality by "divinest Poets Arte."

Drayton concludes his apotheosis of poetry by affirming his laureate aspirations. He will abandon the "Oaten reede" for worthier subject matter. Turning to the heroic, his muse will soar "[a]loft in ayre with Egles wings" (164) and fulfill his pledge to "serve *Idea* in some better steede" (166). Kathleen Tillotson has persuasively argued that Drayton is Spenser's Aetion in *Colin Clouts Come Home Againe* (1595).[6] Drayton's pastoral name Rowland sounds the same as the heroic name Roland, and although it is true of other poets as well, his "Muse" is "full of high thoughts invention" (446).[7]

Drayton's eagerness to win recognition as a poet is a persistent theme throughout *Idea The Shepheards Garland,* but his hope for patronage is explicitly directed toward Mary (Sidney) Herbert. The sixth eclogue begins with a dialogue between Perkin and Gorbo concerning Fortune's cruelty to those who aspire to virtue and achievement. Gorbo asks, "Where been those Nobles" (43) who protected "wise and vertuous men" from "neede and povertie" (27, 28). Only the patronage of those who respect virtuous aspiration can protect humble clients from the vicissitudes of blind fortune. Without this protection, they will be "yswadled in their winding sheete" (47).

These bleak reflections on fortune's hostility to virtue are dispelled by the recollection that Pandora (Countess of Pembroke) continues to act as the patroness of virtue, learning, and poetry. She is the "[w]onder of *Britaine, learnings famous Queene*" (88). Drayton concludes his panegyric by prophesying that after Mary Herbert's death, on her tomb will spring a laurel tree, and from the tree will flow a spring of nectar, "the fountayne of eternall memorie" (150). Drayton's praise of Mary Herbert's virtue insures her "triumph" over "eternitie" (151). Since this panegyric follows a lament over the decline of virtuous patronage, Drayton's inference is clear. The countess is worthy to be the patron of his virtuous muse, and only her patronage will protect and fulfill his promise.

Both the third and eighth eclogues abound with allusions to Spenser and Chaucer, Drayton's laureate masters. He introduces his encomium to Elizabeth I as Beta in the third eclogue by Perkin's remark that Rowland must praise Beta because "learned *Collin*" has gone on a pilgrimage (15). Drayton's imitation of Spenser leads him to use archaic forms, such as "wond" (dwell), "hight" (is named), "cleaped" (named).[8] He pointedly invites comparison with Spenser when his shepherd vows that his courtship will vie with Colin's suit of Rosalind by being "of curtesie the flower" (233).

Although his allusions to Chaucer and Spenser in eclogues 3 and 8 demonstrate Drayton's eagerness to join the tradition of these English laureates, they also establish the premise that poetry flourishes in a golden age and that the bleak present might be transformed into such an age. The eighth eclogue disparages contemporary dramatists as "yonkers," who "rave it out in rime" (5) and laments that "[w]ishes may not revoke that which is past" (114) and bring back the golden age. The classical age of heroic myth and magic is gone. This new, less heroic age offers no subject matter other than the pastoral romance of the country girl Dowsabell and her swain.

Drayton's praise of Elizabeth I as Beta in the third eclogue, however, suggests that past glory can be recaptured, that a new golden age could be brought into being.[9] He concludes his tribute to Elizabeth with a prophecy of empire and Protestant sovereignty:

> And thy large empyre stretch her armes from east unto the west,
> And thou under thy feet mayst tread, that foule seven-headed beast.
>
> (119–20)

Because Beta rules England, the golden age might return. To realize this political promise and social ideal, poets must revere "Idea"; they must resist the worldly temptation to heap "rotten sticks on needles fires" and articulate heroic values for their contemporaries.

Idea The Shepheards Garland, Drayton's early poetic manifesto, asserts his laureate ambitions. His apotheosis of Idea in the fifth eclogue concludes with his promise to turn to heroic verse. He interweaves his literary and social aspirations so that his appeal for patronage is almost indistinguishable from his plea for recognition of his art. Drayton never states, but cleverly implies, that the present could be transformed into a golden age if Pandora (Mary Herbert) decides to support Rowland, a sincere servant of poetry.

Sonnets: *Ideas Mirrour. Amours in Quatorzains*

Ideas Mirrour contains fifty-one poems, or amours, using variations of three or four quatrains, four lines rhyming a b a b or a b b a, concluded by a rhyming couplet. Drayton's sequence appeared with two dedicatory poems: the first is addressed to Anthony Cooke (1559–1604), a landowner near Drayton's birthplace, related to both Francis Bacon and Robert Cecil. In this dedication Drayton claims that he has not "filched" from either Petrarch or Desportes, a "fault too common in thys latter tyme" (12). The concluding line wittily plays on Sidney's well-known boast: "I am no Pickpurse of anothers wit" (14). The second dedication praises Mary (Sidney) Herbert, as Pandora and is signed, *"Gorbo il fidele,"* an allusion to the shepherd who concluded Mary's eulogy in *Idea The Shepheards Garland.* Both of Drayton's dedicatory sonnets invoke the Sidney name.

It might plausibly be argued that Drayton's sonnets are addressed to the muse of poetry or to the Countess of Pembroke or to both muse and countess, but there is no basis for Bernard Newdigate's claim that they are the record of Drayton's "devout Love" for Anne Goodere (42).[10] Newdigate's biographical reading of *Ideas Mirrour* is based on geographical allusions that are subject to more than one interpretation. Drayton concludes his sonnet to Mary Herbert with a reference to the river Anker, which Drayton describes as his Helicon or inspiration in Amour 13: "*Ardens* sweet *Ankor* let thy glory be, / That fayre *Idea* shee doth live by thee" (13–14). Newdigate interprets this reference as an allusion to Anne Goodere because of the mention of the Anker, but Mary Herbert and Lucy Harington, two women from whom Drayton sought patronage in his early poems, had estates on or close enough to the Anker to make the geographical reference uncertain. This particular reference occurs in a commendatory poem unmistakably intended for Mary

Herbert, but the identification of Idea as Anne Goodere has been delivered with such conviction that the unwary can be misled. Recently, a historian writing about patronage commented: "The bond must have been all the stronger when reader and patron were one and the same for the poet was now likely to tailor the poem to a closer, more personal fit, as in the case of Drayton's sonnets for Lady Rainsford (Anne Goodere)."[11] The insistent biographical interpretation of Drayton's work has prevented critics from approaching his pastoral and sonnet sequence as clever, inventive bids for patronage by a promising poet.

Drayton has rarely been compared with John Donne, but this comparison illuminates the intellectual nature of his conceits. In 1594 he soberly tries to extend conventions that Donne mockingly inverts, but, like Donne, uses a wide range of subject matter. In Amour 11 his persona is taught the "Alphabet of love" by his mistress (1). Most of the lessons concern phonology because Drayton alludes to "vowels," "consonants," "liquids," and "mutes." In Amour 24 he turns to geography. When his persona receives a phonology or geography lesson from his mistress, the incongruity of the lesson is justified, not parodied. When he allows wit to color his conceits, as in Amour 6, paralleling his mistress and a phoenix, the concluding line, "So maist thou live, past world, past fame, past end," treats the conceit seriously (14). In *Ideas Mirrour* he tries to adapt his conceits to Petrarchan conventions, but these attempts frequently fail.

Ideas Mirrour did succeed in furnishing his contemporaries with fodder for satiric cannon fire. In Amour 8 Drayton tried to turn Neoplatonic number symbolism into a courtly compliment based on witty computation. The first eight lines offer examples of how threes and nines combine. With praiseworthy exactitude, his mistress joins the nine Worthies in the ninth line:

> My Worthie, one to these nine Worthies, addeth,
>   And my faire Muse, one Muse unto the nine;
>   And my good Angell in my soule divine,
>   With one more order, these nine orders gladdeth.
> My Muse, my Worthy, and my Angell then,
> Makes every one of these three nines a ten.
>
>   (9–14)

Shortly after Drayton's *Ideas Mirrour* appeared in 1594, Sir John Davies, a law student at the Middle Temple, wrote an epigram entitled "In Decium" (to the tenth) satirizing the decorum of Drayton's arithmetic:

> Audacious Painters have nine worthies made,
> But Poet Decius more audacious farre,
> Making his mistres march with men of warre,
> With title of tenth worthie doth her lade;
> > Me thinkes that gul did use his termes as fit,
> > Which termde his love a Giant for hir wit.
>
> (1–6)

Davies's epigram ridicules Drayton's introduction of his mistress into the company of the Nine Worthies and plays upon his presumption in associating himself with the Sidneys. He reclassifies him as the clown in Sidney's *Arcadia,* who also violates decorum. That Davies specifically intended to satirize Drayton is confirmed by Ben Jonson's conversations with William Drummond of Hawthornden.[12]

Joseph Hall more sharply satirized Drayton in book 6 of *Virgidemiae.* He first ridicules Drayton's description of poetic inspiration:

> For he can tell how fury reft his sense,
> And Phoebus fill'd him with intelligence.

Then Hall accuses Drayton of filching "whole pages at a clap . . . [f]rom honest Petrarch, clad in English weed," of using too many hyphenated adjectives, and of naming the spirit of Sidney without due respect.[13] Drayton's response to this satire is revealing. He defends the decorum of his numerology in *Endimion and Phoebe. Ideas Latmus* (1595), his next published poem, and he revises but retains Amour 8 in every edition of his sonnets, even in his last version *Idea* (1619). Drayton was as thin-skinned about literary ridicule as he was about social slights.

In *Ideas Mirrour* Drayton began his long apprenticeship as a literary artist. The promise, which was to be more fully realized in his splendid *Idea* (1619), is suggested by Amour 31. Sitting alone, the poet is urged by Love to write and by Reason to desist from such folly. The allegorical debate between Love and Reason is resolved in the couplet; the poet acknowledges, that "Love alone finds reason in my love" (14). Irony builds in the preceding quatrains toward the concluding paradox. Drayton retained this poem in successive editions, reprinting it in 1619 as it had first appeared in 1594.

Minor Epic: *Endimion and Phoebe. Ideas Latmus*

Endimion and Phoebe, a 1,032-line poem in rhymed couplets, retells the myth of the shepherd Endymion who falls in love with the goddess of the moon. The genre to which *Endimion and Phoebe* belongs has been labeled the minor epic, Ovidian verse, erotic narrative, mythological narrative, Elizabethan narrative, and epyllion (episode from an epic).[14] This genre was very popular in the last decades of the sixteenth century and produced works such as Shakespeare's *Venus and Adonis,* Marlowe's *Hero and Leander,* and George Chapman's continuation of Marlowe's poem. Although Drayton adopts Marlowe's rhymed couplets, he turned to du Bartas and Ficino rather than to Ovid for his inspiration. Du Bartas's *L'Uranie, ou Muse Celeste* had been translated into English by James I in 1584 and into Latin by Robert Ashley in 1589. Drayton fills *Endimion and Phoebe* with accounts of the planets, an aerial journey, and two visions, Neoplatonic motifs that also appear in Du Bartas's *L'Uranie.*

Endimion and Phoebe (1595) is dedicated to Lucy Harington Russell, Countess of Bedford, who in 1594 at age thirteen had married Edward Russell, Earl of Bedford.[15] Metaphorically, Lucy is Drayton's Phoebe, his inspirational light. His dedication promises: "And but thy selfe, no subject will I aske" (12). The dedication and the wordplay on Lucy's name suggest that on one level we may read *Endimion and Phoebe* as an allegorical statement about Drayton's patronage relationship with the countess. Endymion falls in love with the beautiful and virtuous Phoebe, who skillfully guides him up the Platonic ladder. When she delivers a chaste kiss, Endymion, transformed by divine inspiration, becomes a poet. Like Endymion, Drayton has learned art from his patroness (561). Endymion's inspired tribute to Phoebe is also Drayton's tribute to the Countess of Bedford. This eulogy echoes and elaborates on imagery in Drayton's dedicatory sonnet to Lucy: "My vitall spirit, receves his spirit from thee" (573); "Thou nourishest the flame wherein I burne" (577).

At the conclusion of the poem Endymion is granted not one, but two visions. In the first, he is carried aloft into the heavens where he is shown the principles of harmony that govern the universe. Thus far, scholars argue, Drayton's objective is to present either an allegory of poetic inspiration or of Neoplatonic ecstasy.[16] Neither of these interpretations of *Endimion and Phoebe,* however, explains why Drayton makes the second vision a processional masque or triumph. He tells us "now great *Phoebe* in her tryumph came" (823) and lists the many "tytles of her glorious name" (824). The list ranges from familiar to less familiar epithets, from Diana, Delia, and Cynthia to Prothiria, Dictinna, and Proserpine. Drayton concludes this list with the line: "*Latona,* and *Lucina,* most divine" (828). The list of epithets for Phoebe concludes with a complimentary play on the name Lucy as "Lucina," an association Ben Jonson also makes.[17]

The conclusion of *Endimion and Phoebe* contains a tribute to a "sweet mayd" who is associated with the "Nymph of *Ankor*" (1,011; 1,014). Combe Abbey, one of the Harington estates, was located on the Anker. The tribute to Idea closely follows and extends Drayton's dedicatory sonnet to Lucy. *Endimion and Phoebe*, because it is consciously allegorical, invites multiple interpretations. On one level, Drayton intended *Endimion and Phoebe* to compliment Lucy by suggesting that his chaste admiration for her beauty and wisdom had inspired his verse. Phoebe is the source of inspiration for Endymion; her platonic kiss awakens the fire that makes him a poet. Phoebe is also the subject of Drayton's poem. Drayton thus makes Lucy the source of inspiration and the subject of that inspiration. The line in his dedicatory sonnet in which he claims "And but thy selfe, no subject will I aske" is elucidated by the poem.

Tragical Complaints (1593–1594)

While the complaint poems of the 1590s derive from the *Mirror for Magistrates,* Drayton's complaints are a curious amalgam of the tradition spawned by that older work and the newer Ovidian minor epic. The focus of the Mirror tradition was political. The title of Richard II suggests how the complaints were to be read: "How kyng Richarde the seconde was for his evyll governaunce deposed from his seat, and miserably murdred in prison."[18] In the 1590s Drayton was unsure of whether to align his poems with the Mirror or the Ovidian tradition. He describes *Peirs Gaveston* (1593) as a "tragicall discourse" and *Matilda* (1594) as a "tragicall Historie" (158, 211). Both complaints are introduced by the ghosts of historical figures who return after death to lament the events that led to their tragic ends. Since neither the complaint nor the minor epic was a well-defined canonical genre, a poet working with these forms in the 1590s was faced, not by rules, but by a series of critical choices. The poet had to select from among a variety of possible models and narrative modes. The problem of achieving a unified effect was partially rhetorical. The author had to adopt an identifiable and coherent stance in relationship to the reader.[19]

Drayton's early tragical complaints lack this coherence. *Peirs Gaveston* is filled with apostrophes that bewail the cruelty of fortune and yet are frankly erotic. Edward I, capably assisted by his son surnamed the Black Prince, pushed back the militant Scots from England's borders and laid claim to a huge amount of French territory. Edward II lost these lands and alienated the old nobility by elevating his male favorites above them.

Drayton buries most of these historical facts in rhetorical flourishes. The poem begins by praising the court of Edward I as a school where arts, arms, and gentility reign. The "rarest excellence" of Edward I finds its counterpart in *"Englands Beta"* (57, 55), Drayton's epithet for Elizabeth in *Idea The Shepheards Garland*. To repay Gaveston's father for his service in arms, Edward I makes Gaveston his son's page. After this fact is communicated, the poem leaves history behind and becomes unabashedly erotic. Gaveston's beauty assumes cosmic proportions as he appears like an "after world of wonders" (150), a "death-presaging comet" (152). Hyphenated adjectives are piled upon each other as superlative follows superlative. No skilled artist ("cunning'st pensill-man," 157) could have traced such an image. Not even Platonic poetry can do justice to Gaveston's charms:

> Or the divine *Idea* of the thought
> With rare descriptions of high poesy,
>   Should all compose a body and a mind,
>   Such a one seem'd I, the wonder of my kind.
>   (159–62)

Gaveston plays *"Ganimed"* to Prince Edward's *"Jove"* (213). The eroticism of their relationship is elaborated in mythological allusions (240–43) and metaphors (233–34) that stress physical sexuality:

> Nature had taught my tongue her perfect time,
> Which in his eare stroake duely as a chyme.
>   (251–52)

Gaveston exclaims:

> I waxt his winges and taught him art to flye,
> Who on his back might beare me through the skye.
>   (281–82)

Laments over sin and ill fortune periodically intrude upon their delights, but both Gaveston and Edward are presented sympathetically.[20]

After Edward becomes king, the barons insist that Gaveston be banished. Edward II experiences "hart-kylling griefe" (975), "death-thirsting rage"

(977), "sky-covering clowdes" (979), and "blood-drying sicknes" (981). He curses his crown and then cries out that a king "should ever privilege his pleasure" (107). While the barons accuse Gaveston of exhausting the treasury and bewitching the king, we are not asked to share their negative portrait of Gaveston.

Edward II remains constant in his love for his male favorite. Gaveston loves Edward, but he also loves his wife, Edward's pure niece. Her chastity affords Drayton the opportunity to insert an incongruous tribute to Elizabeth's chastity (691–702). The least explicable lapse in point of view occurs at the conclusion of *Peirs Gaveston* (1,717–40). Gaveston has just described Edward's grief over his death. Without any shift in persona, Gaveston's ghost says that he will go to the river Anker and "unto chaste *Idea* tell my care" (1,719) and then return to the "faire *Elisian* plaine" and carve "*Ideas* sacred name" on the "Trees of never dying fame" (1,727–28). The narrative logic is confused: why is Gaveston discussing Idea?

Even though *Peirs Gaveston* reads like a poem in search of a genre, a focus, and a point of view, it has great energy. As is true of most of Drayton's early work, it is not difficult to pick out highly quotable lines. In spite of the lack of coherence in *Peirs Gaveston* and *Matilda*, both poems have a certain appeal. Those of Drayton's contemporaries who relished John Lyly's *Euphues* (1579) would have responded just as favorably to the rhetorical exuberance of Drayton's tragical complaints.

Mortimeriados

Mortimeriados (1596), a 2,912-line poem in rhyme royal, like *Peirs Gaveston,* deals with the history of the reign of Edward II. In *Mortimeriados* Edward has married Isabel of France, but continues to prefer male favorites. Isabel finds solace in the arms of Robert Mortimer, Lord Wigmore, whom Drayton portrays as a great-souled hero. The poem describes the wars between the king and the barons, Edward's enforced abdication in favor of his son, Edward III, and Edward III's overthrow of Mortimer.

Mortimeriados was entered in the Stationer's Register on 15 April 1596 and appeared with the most effusive dedication that Drayton ever wrote. His *Endimion and Phoebe* (1595) may not have been successful as a Neoplatonic allegory, but it must have been warmly received by Lucy. The dedicatory fourteen-line sonnet to *Endimion and Phoebe* becomes in *Mortimeriados* a sixty-three-line poem in rhyme royal. This poem proclaims "unto ages yet to come, / Whilst *Bedford* lyv'd, what lyving *Bedford* was" (57–58). Drayton's message comes at the conclusion of the dedication when he pointedly remarks that his poem will "shewe what thy great power could bring to passe" (61). Drayton had received "sweet golden showers" from Lucy for *Endimion and Phoebe; Mortimeriados* was his demonstration that her patronage had borne fruit. He interrupts the narrative of *Mortimeriados* twice to invoke Lucy as his muse (260–66 and 2,080–87).

He appears to have considered *Mortimeriados* the worthier effort of his pen that he had promised in *Idea The Shepheards Garland*. He moves in the direction of epic by introducing epic similes, catalogs of nobles, remarkably vivid battle scenes, and other epic conventions. In spite of the addition of these epic trappings, *Mortimeriados* more closely resembles his earlier tragical complaints than it does an epic. His contemporaries probably agreed; Francis Meres classifies it as a tragedy, not an epic, in his *Palladis Tamia*.[21] Drayton's Mortimer unquestionably figures as the hero; his great-souled vision and military prowess command respect: "The towring pitch wherein he flew for fame, / Declar'd the ayrie whence the Eagle came" (76–77). Every effort is made to display Mortimer's virtue. At the conclusion of the poem, when the young Edward III surprises Mortimer in Isabel's chambers, Mortimer is allowed to defend himself eloquently. He regrets that he did not die on the battlefield, giving Drayton an opportunity to remind us of his military prowess, and urges the queen's son to let him absorb all of his vengeance. Drayton does not include a response from Edward III, but we learn that Mortimer was not allowed to answer the charges brought against him at his trial.

Isabel is a motiveless monster in the chronicle histories, but Drayton invites our sympathy for her. Richard Hardin has observed that in John Stow's *Annals of England* (1592), Isabel is described as torturing Hugh Spencer, her husband's favorite, before she executes him without a trial.[22] Later she orders the murder of her husband and king. Drayton does compare Isabel with Medea, merciless enough to tear her "Brothers lymmes" (661), but she does not authorize the murder of her husband. Comparison with Stow is especially enlightening because, in the notes to *Peirs Gaveston* (1593), Drayton claims to have consulted Stow's library. Unlike Stow, he portrays Isabel as deeply in love with Mortimer.

With considerable political naiveté Drayton shows that Edward II was responsible for many of his own misfortunes. Few concessions are made to the sacred nature of kingship. When Edward II assents to his deposition under duress, he reminds the barons that he is the king by "heaven's decree" (1,713), observing that his lawless acts may jeopardize their allegiance but insisting that they may not uncrown a king (1,715). Before his murders dispatch him, Drayton portrays him as reading the chronicle histories of English kings; cursing his birth, he movingly pleads, "only be it forgot that ere I was"

(2,016). We pity Edward because of the way he dies, but Drayton takes care to be sure that our respect is reserved for Mortimer.

After his trial and before his execution, Mortimer takes leave of the queen in a letter in which he insists that he loved Edward III like his own son. He prays that future ages will only sing Isabel's praise and that her fame will last longer than the Tower which she has named after him (2,689–2,751). Mortimer's epistolary farewell anticipates Drayton's use of the epistle as a genre in *Englands Heroicall Epistles* (1597).

Tragical Complaints

In 1596 Drayton published revised versions of *Peirs Gaveston and Matilda,* and added a new tragical complaint, *Robert of Normandy.* The complaints of 1596 are dedicated to Lucy, Countess of Bedford, "as a monument of the zeale I beare to your vertues" and in recognition of Lucy's "bountie" (249). In the dedication, Drayton, as in *Endimion and Phoebe,* plays upon Lucy's name: "The light I have, is borrowed from your beams, which Envie shall not eclipse, so long as you shall favourablie shine" (249).

In 1596 Drayton had not yet arrived at a stable conception of the complaint as a genre. He added rhetorical flourishes to his already heavily embellished poems: twenty-five new stanzas to *Peirs Gaveston* and twenty-six to *Matilda.* These early poems suggest how Drayton worked. He experimented with a particular genre or tradition and published the resulting poem. He continued to experiment and revise his published poems and then republished them later with new material. There are two or more versions for nearly all of Drayton's early work. Because these revisions take place over a number of years, his work is unsuited to exposition by discrete genres or poems except within a chronological framework.

Drayton's apprenticeship, 1591–97, did not produce a single poem that has received unqualified critical approval, but in this early work we glimpse the potential that he was to realize fully in *Englands Heroicall Epistles.*

Chapter Three
Englands Heroicall Epistles

The promise of Drayton's early work comes to fruition in *Englands Heroicall Epistles*. He recognized the quality of this work and, as a result, never subjected it to minute revision. In 1597 the poem consisted of eighteen fictional letters in rhymed couplets. Drayton explains that the epistles are called *Englands Heroicall Epistles* because the nine historical couples who exchange letters are English or else "their loves were obtained" in England (2:130).[1] He observes that he does not want his poems to be regarded as "Braynish," unduly passionate or erotic, and that consequently he has "inter-woven Matters Historicall" (2:130). The epistolary genre allows him to circumscribe his fictions with a historical framework.

Drayton acknowledges that the literary antecedent of *Englands Heroicall Epistles* is Ovid's *Heroides,* but then parenthetically observes "whose Imitator I partly professe to be" (2:130). He takes little from Ovid except the concept of a collection of verse epistles; the *Heroides* and *Englands Heroicall Epistles* belong to the same genre, but are fundamentally different poems.[2] In the first fifteen of Ovid's *Heroides* women write letters to their absent lovers; the elegiac tone varies subtly as one heroine after another laments her lost love.[3] In the last six paired epistles the predominant tone is optimistic.[4] The sophisticated Paris and more innocent Acontius will successfully seduce Helen and Cydippe; Hero and Leander face only the physical obstacle of the Hellespont. Since tragedy awaits these lovers, their present confidence is shadowed by pathos.

Two rhetorical forms dominate the *Heroides:* the *ethopoeia,* a speech or letter written by a historical or mythological figure at a decisive moment; and the *suasoria,* a speech or letter that attempts to persuade or influence the person addressed. Ovid most frequently uses the *suasoria;* persuasion is explicit or implicit in nearly every epistle. Drayton only obliquely uses the *suasoria;* he favors the *encomium,* a set of formulas for praise, and the *blazon,* a catalog of the physical charms of the beloved.[5]

Instead of imitating Ovid's unity and subtle variations in tone, Drayton strives for variety and contrast. His heroines have not been abandoned by their lovers; external circumstances bring unhappiness to Queen Isabel and

Mortimer as well as to Guilford Dudley and Lady Jane Grey. Two of Drayton's many departures from the *Heroides* are especially innovative: the generic variety that he brings to the verse epistle and the historical materials that he introduces to avoid seeming "braynish." Of these two, Drayton's adaptation of historical materials is more important for interpreting this poem and understanding the repercussions that it had on his later career. Nevertheless, the ordering of the epistles in 1597 and in successive editions affects the reader's reaction to *Englands Heroicall Epistles*. Drayton deliberately begins with two innocuous sets of epistles that, as he observes in his notes to King John, contain "no particular Points of Historie, more then the generalitie of the Argument layeth open" (2:158). After these amatory epistles, the poems become increasingly political in their references, as we approach the present.

The first two sets of epistles between Rosamond and Henry II (1154–89) and Henry's son King John (1199–1216) and Matilda illustrate how Drayton's early generic experimentation contributed to his technique. He enriches the historical narrative by borrowing conventions from the Petrarchan sonnet, the Elizabethan minor epic, and the historical complaint. An English king and his mistress are surrounded by statues, embroidered tapestries, and caskets as pregnant with literary allusions as those we find in Shakespeare's *Rape of Lucrece* or Marlowe's *Hero and Leander*. Drayton repeatedly uses *ekphrasis,* an extended description of a work of art; Rosamond's emotions are conveyed by her reactions to external objects. When Rosamond sees a painting of Lucrece in her gallery, the image of chaste Lucrece reminds her of her own guilt. In the garden she recalls her lost chastity when she sees a statue of "Naked *Diana* in the Fountaine" (141); she is pursued by her own unhappy thoughts as fiercely as Actaeon was pursued by his hounds (143). This sequence of accusing mythological images externalizes Rosamond's internal guilt. The night before she loses her honor, Henry sends her a casket covered with mythological scenes of seduction; the images warn her of his intentions and foreshadow her submission.

Drayton repeats and reinterprets images presented in one epistle in its paired epistle. When Rosamond goes to fish in a stream, the hook reminds her that she swallowed the bait that was laid for her. Henry, too, mentions the stream and fish, but he believes that the fish will be so amazed by Rosamond's beauty that they will forget to feed. The mythological images that externalize Rosamond's guilt are reinterpreted by Henry to accommodate his desire. Because the epistles are linked in this way, we read them reflexively as commentaries on each other. The parallelism of the letters exposes Henry's rationalization of his liaison with Rosamond. He knows that his wife Elinor's jealousy threatens his mistress, but balks at admitting that his attentions have made Rosamond unhappy.

In addition to using parallelism to contrast states of mind in paired epistles, Drayton extends this technique to the overall structure of *Englands Heroicall Epistles*. Henry II and John woo women whom they wish as mistresses, but their parallel circumstances serve only to heighten contrasts in tone. King Henry suffers like a Petrarchan lover when Rosamond resists him. Although, like Romeo, Henry offers to change his name if it offends Rosamond, unlike Romeo, he is an older man, lonely and burdened with his responsibilities as a ruler. King John, like Leander in Marlowe's *Hero and Leander* (1593), employs all the casuistry of a Renaissance logician to woo Matilda. He delivers a *blazon* that catalogs Matilda's charms and concludes by sensually inverting the sacred and the profane:

> Ile be thy Servant, and my Bed thy Shrine.
> When I doe offer, be thy Brest the Altar,
> And when I pray, thy Mouth shall be my Psalter.
> (84–86)

Parodying the religious imagery that Romeo and Juliet and many other Petrarchan lovers employ, John deliberately ignores Matilda's religious sensibility. Borrowing from *Matilda* (1594), his complaint poem about these same figures, Drayton shows us that only lust motivates John. He sneers at Matilda's bleak future in the convent, but she replies that if Rosamond had taken the holy veil, she could have avoided being hidden away like the "ugly Minotaur" (169). Allusions link the epistles of Rosamond and Matilda, as they do others that follow, inviting us to compare characters and their relationships. Through his techniques of parallelism and contrast, Drayton achieves more complex judgments than the simple morals offered in the earlier sequence of historical portraits in *The Mirror for Magistrates*. He, for example, does not contrast Rosamond's license with Matilda's chastity. The reader is led to sympathize with Rosamond's suffering because she is deeply repentant. Matilda earns our admiration, but it is Rosamond whom we pity. Drayton fully exploits fictional artifice to stimulate complex assessments of historical figures.

The epistolary mode affects both the rhetorical stance of the author of each epistle and the tone of the work as a whole. We as readers are aware of Rosamond's letter as a text but also of her relationship to Henry, the audience to whom the letter is directed. We realize that Rosamond's letter is not a dramatic monologue, that it is a written text. The tone of this address will be private, more so than forensic or deliberative rhetorical modes in which a speaker addresses an unknown audience. But because the letter is written, and we are conscious of its being written, the tone will be less intimate and immediate than the private conversations we overhear in John Donne's *Songs and Sonnets.* The author's emotions are inscribed in the text. As readers, we are distanced from the speaker by th2 formal existence of this text and also by our awareness of the historical importance of the speakers. This distance allows Drayton to employ more heightened rhetoric than would be appropriate in a sonnet. As a genre, the verse epistle was ideally suited to his rhetorical virtuosity.

His contemporaries immediately responded to his achievement in *Englands Heroicall Epistles.* He had interwoven history and fiction while making a distinctive literary contribution to a relatively unexplored genre. Five separate editions appeared between 1597 and 1602. Altogether *Englands Heroicall Epistles* went through seven editions between 1596 and 1609 while only one edition of Spenser's *Faerie Queene* appeared in the same time period. That Drayton used English history as a context for his epistles contributed to their popularity. His audience viewed history as a "mirror" in which magistrates and other men could see the past reflected and test their perceptions of the present. George Puttenham praises historical poetry because it can present a "lively image" of virtue.[6] He equates history with individual memory, observing that "the present time and things so swiftly passe away, as they give us no leasure almost to looke into them and much lesse to know and consider of them."[7] Wholesale agreement that the past offered a commentary on the present conditioned Drayton's audience to approach historical poetry as political commentary. History instructed because it illuminated the present.

Englands Heroicall Epistles did not appear in a vacuum; its timeliness helps to account for its popularity, but because its specific historical context has been ignored, this extremely popular collection of poems has never been interpreted as it was by Drayton's contemporaries and patrons.[8] The most recent full-length study of Drayton's work, and the only one to comment on the historical thrust of *Englands Heroicall Epistles,* describes the poem as showing "divine Providence guiding England through a troublesome past into a glorious present under Elizabeth."[9] Although history is alluded to, this reading of *Englands Heroicall Epistles* removes the text from history by ignoring its own historical context, as was the fashion during the vogue of "new criticism." No attention is paid to bibliographical facts. In 1597 *Englands Heroicall Epistles* contained nine paired epistles. In 1598 Drayton added five new ones. It was not until 1599 that this poem contained the twelve epistles that are identified as supporting the Tudor myth.[10] *Englands Heroicall Epistles* typically has been interpreted in a privileged literary world into which politics, patronage, and even its own bibliographical history are not allowed to intrude.

Writing about English history carried with its certain risks in the late 1590s, especially for a poet who hoped to gain preferment by his pen. On 1 June 1599, printers were forbidden to print any work of English history unless it had been authorized by a member of the Privy Council.[11] In spite of the risks to which historical materials exposed authors, plays and poetry hinting at political topicality were assured of an audience. An author who wished to succeed in the complex system governing literary clientage, however, had to be sensitive to what could safely be suggested and alert to the political implications that might be read into his work.

Drayton's preface to *Englands Heroicall Epistles* and his Horatian epigraph indicate that he understood the risk posed by misinterpretation:

Seeing these Epistles are now at length made publique, it is imagined that I ought to be accountable to the worlde of my private meaning, chiefly for mine own discharge, lest being mistaken, I fall in hazard of a just and universall Reprehension: for,

> —*Hae nugae seria ducent*
> *In mala derisum semel exceptumque sinistre.* (2:130)[12]

He edges away from taking responsibility for the interpretation of his poems, but his attempts to be disarming probably had the opposite effect. In sections of the preface that were later deleted he offers to explain "why I observe not the persons dignity in the dedication" (Tillotson, 101), but his explanation becomes so tortuous syntactically that it functions as a one-sentence obfuscation:

. . . seeing none to whom I have dedicated any two Epistles but have their states overmatched by them who are made to speak in the Epistles, how ever the order is in dedication, yet in respect of theyr degrees in my devotion, and the cause before recited, I hope they suffer no disparagement, seeing every one is the first in theyr particuler interest, having in some sort, sorted the complection of the Epistles, to the character of theyr judgments to whom I dedicate them, excepting only the blamefulnes of the persons passion, in those points wherein the passion is blameful. (Tillotson, 101–2)

Drayton's motive for making this statement is hardly transparent. At first, he appears concerned about not having ranked the dedicatees in terms of social status, but then announces that he has "sorted the complection of the Epistles, to the character of theyr judgments to whom [he] dedicates them." He qualifies this fairly straightforward statement by saying that his dedicatees are exempted from "the blamefulnes of the persons passion, in those points wherein the passion is blameful" (Tillotson, 102). Was Drayton concerned about ordering his dedications in a manner that might offend the class consciousness of a person of rank, or was he concerned about dedicating politically volatile material to dedicatees who had not seen these texts and might be offended?

His clarification muddies the issue further by implying that he should not be held responsible either for the order of the dedications or for the association of a dedicatee with any particular epistle: "Lastly, such manifest difference being betwixt every one of them, where or howsoever they be marshaled, how can I be justly appeached of unadvisement" (Tillotson, 102). He concludes the preface with yet another disclaimer: "If they be as harmlessly taken as I meant them it shal suffice to have onely touched the cause of the title of the dedications" (Tillotson, 102). In the 1597 preface to *Englands Heroicall Epistles* Drayton invites his readers to connect his dedicatees with figures and incidents in English history, claiming that he has matched "the complection of the Epistles" to the "character" of the dedicatees' "judgments." This invitation insured that the historical design of *Englands Heroicall Epistles* would receive careful scrutiny.

Drayton intended his first edition of *Englands Heroicall Epistles* as a major bid for patronage. His previous work had appeared with no more than one dedication. This poem contains no fewer than nine dedications, one for each set of epistles, but Drayton remains most interested in the patronage of Edward Russell, Earl of Bedford, and his wife Lucy. In 1597 the dedications and the nine pairs of epistles were ordered as the following list suggests. The dedications precede the epistles that they accompany; the authors of the epistles are italicized, and the first name given indicates who began the exchanges of letters.

1) Dedication to Lucy Harington Russell, Countess of Bedford
   Rosamond and King Henry II (1154–89)

2) Dedication to William Parker, fourth Baron Monteagle (succeeded to this title through his mother, daughter and heir of William Stanley, third Lord Monteagle); eldest son of Edward Parker, tenth Baron Morley
   King John (1199–1216), son of Henry II, and Matilda

3)   Dedication to Anne, Lady Harington, mother of the Countess of Bedford
      Queen Isabel of France, wife of Edward II, and Roger Mortimer, eighth Baron of
      Wigmore (1324)

4)   Dedication to Edward Russell, Earl of Bedford
      Queen Isabel and Richard II (1399)

5)   Dedication to Lord Henry Howard (1540–1614), second son of Henry
      Howard, Earl of Surrey
      Queen Katherine, widow of Henry V, and Owen Tudor (1429)

6)   Dedication to Elizabeth Tanfield
      Queen Margaret, wife of Henry VI, and William de la Pole (1450)

7)   Dedication to Sir Thomas Mounson
      Edward IV and Mistress Shore (1470)

8)   Dedication to Henry Goodere, Esquire
      Mary Tudor, Queen of France, and Charles Brandon, Duke of Suffolk (1515)

9)   Dedication to Mistress Frances Goodere, daughter to Sir Henry Goodere,
      Knight and wife to Henry Goodere, Esquire
      Guilford Dudley and Lady Jane Grey (1554)

To understand the impact of *Englands Heroicall Epistles* in the late 1590s, we need to consider what principles governed Drayton's selection of these particular historical couples. First, in 1597 every interchange involves at least one monarch and frequently two. Second, each set of epistles, after the first two, concerns the deposition of a monarch (the reigns of Edward II, Richard II, and Henry VI) or is related to a struggle over succession to the throne. To write about deposition was hazardous; to comment on the succession was legally prohibited.

Elizabeth's failure to name a successor alarmed her subjects. Rival claimants might plunge England into civil war after her death. Memories of the War of the Roses, a long and bloody struggle over succession to the throne, were still fresh. Drayton's generation had also matured when Catholic Spain was conspiring to eradicate Protestantism.[13] The possibility of a Catholic succession engineered by Spain alarmed militant Protestants who associated Catholicism with the suppression of humanist inquiry.

The succession question was especially volatile in 1597. In 1571 an act prohibiting the publication of claims to the throne not established by Parliament was passed. The stalwart Puritan Peter Wentworth, whose *A Pithie Exhortation to Her Majestie for establishing her successor to the crowne* had been drafted in 1587, revised his tract in order to raise the succession question in the Parliament of 1593.[14] When the queen and Privy Council learned that

Wentworth had attracted parliamentary supporters, he was sent to the Tower of London and his co-conspirators to Fleet Prison. Wentworth, who was sixty-nine, remained in the Tower until he died in 1597, the year that *Englands Heroicall Epistles* first appeared in print. Wentworth's *Pithie Exhortation* was printed posthumously in 1598, the year that Drayton added five new epistles to his poem.

Drayton's preface, his selection of historical materials, and his ordering of the epistles invited political interpretation, but the texts of the epistles themselves would have convinced his audience that Drayton was using history to comment on the present.

Third Set: Queen Isabel and Mortimer (1324)

Drayton was very familiar with the historical background of the Isabel-Mortimer epistles. The reign of Edward II (1307–27) was the subject of Marlowe's play *Edward II* (1592–93) and of Drayton's own *Peirs Gaveston* (1593–96), *Mortimeriados* (1596), and *The Barons Warres* (1603). Edward II's wife, Isabel, daughter of Philip of France, turns to Roger Mortimer, eighth Baron of Wigmore, when Edward prefers male favorites. Mortimer leads the barons in an uprising against the king, but the rebellion fails and Mortimer is imprisoned in the Tower. Drayton begins his epistles in 1324 after Mortimer has escaped and fled to France. Isabel and Mortimer exchange their letters before they succeed in deposing and murdering Edward.

Although she rages at Edward II for publicly preferring his male favorites, Drayton's Isabel is not merely a jealous woman outraged by her mate's sexual preferences. She scorns Edward's economic mismanagement, blaming his councillors for giving him poor advice. She draws an unflattering portrait of Edward II, whom she claims is too distracted by his favorites to pursue an aggressive foreign policy (2.57–130).

Isabel's censure was not unfamiliar to Drayton's contemporaries. The Jesuit Robert Parsons had issued a series of political tracts using English history as a gloss on contemporary politics. Under the pseudonym Doleman, his *A Conference about the Next Succession* appeared in 1594 with arguments justifying the proposition that "Princes may for good cause be deposed."[15] Parsons argued that God had "allowed and assisted the same, with good success to the weale publicque," citing as evidence the reigns of Edward II, Richard II, Henry VI (F4v). Parson's work was not only outlawed in England, but a house-to-house search was also conducted to seize hidden copies.

In *A Conference* Parsons reiterated his suspicion of Elizabeth's trusted treasurer, William Cecil, Lord Burghley, and his son Sir Robert Cecil, whom he had described as early as 1592 as "farr more noysome and pernitios to the realme, then ever were the *Spencers, Peeter of Gaverstone,* or any that ever abused either Prince or people."[16] Early in her reign Elizabeth was criticized for listening to her favorites, rather than to her wise councillors. In the 1590s this criticism was revived but with a new twist. The supporters of Robert Devereux, Earl of Essex, charged that Elizabeth favored the Cecils, greedy men of vulgar breeding, over the old nobility, as had Richard II.

Drayton endows Roger Mortimer with the heroic virtues that he most admired. He stresses Mortimer's chivalry, a trait identified with Essex, and Mortimer's military prowess, the source of much of Essex's popularity. During military expeditions to France (1591), Cadiz (1596), the Islands Voyage (1597), and Ireland (1599) Essex persisted in antagonizing Elizabeth by knighting men who distinguished themselves on the field. Those whom he knighted naturally felt a special allegiance to Essex. Sir Anthony Shirley, who served under Essex at Rouen, resolved to let him be "the pattern of my civil life, and from him to draw a worthy model of all my actions."[17] Drayton's Mortimer, like Essex, behaves as a chivalric commander, committed to noble deeds.

Mortimer, like Essex, has a noble background. Proudly alluding to his grandfather's having reestablished King Arthur's Round Table at Kenilworth, Mortimer pays tribute to chivalry:

> Whose Princely Order honour'd *England* more,
> Then all the Conquests she achiev'd before.
> (57–58)

Mortimer patriotically longs to subjugate France and Scotland for the glory of England; he envisions the establishment of a great English empire:

> O[u]r well-rig'd Ships shall stretch their swelling Wings,
> And drag their Anchors through the sandie Fome,
> About the World in ev'ry Clime to rome,
> And those unchrist'ned Countries call our owne,
> Where scarce the Name of *England* hath been knowne.
> (78–82)

Drayton was inspired by the vision of a great empire won by exploration and heroic conquest. For his generation, heroic achievement was associated with Sir Philip Sidney and then with Essex, who believed England should pursue a militant foreign policy.

In a witty bilingual pun on his own name Mortimer says that the name of his house will disappear into the dead sea before any Mortimer will ever humble himself to a king:

> And in the dead Sea sinke our Houses Fame,
> From Whose vaste Depth we first deriv'd our Name;
> Before foule blacke-mouth'd Infamie shall sing,
> That *Mortimer* ere stoop'd unto a King.
>
> (83–86)

Mortimer's witty Ovidian pun gallantly defines his courage. At the conclusion of his epistle Drayton allows Mortimer to refer to Edward's deposition:

> Our Warlike Sword shall drive him from his Throne,
> Where he shall lye for us to tread upon.
>
> (137–38)

Although the deposition of Richard II was more frequently offered as an analogy to Elizabeth's overthrow, a reign as remote as that of Edward II could still have relevance for an Elizabethan. Lord Burghley left a six-page manuscript dated 1595, containing notes on the reign of Edward II and marking enemies of the Crown.[18]

Drayton dedicated the Isabel-Mortimer epistles to Anne, Lady Harington, Lucy's mother. Prudently, he does not link her with the formidable and adulterous Isabel; instead he associates Lady Harington's worth with Mortimer's strength of character. Her "worth" and "pure fire" recall Mortimer's fiery courage: "Worth is best discerned by the worthy, dejected mindes want that pure fire which should give vigor to vertue" (Tillotson, 107). By connecting Mortimer and Lady Harington, Drayton confirmed that the epistles and dedicatees might be related.

Fourth Set: Queen Isabel and Richard II

Richard II (1377–99) was the grandson of Edward III and the only son of Edward the Black Prince, the Plantagenets who conquered France. He married Anne of Bohemia in 1382; after she died in 1394, he married Isabel, the eleven-year-old daughter of Charles of France, in 1396. Richard was deposed on 29 September 1399 by Henry Bullingbrook, Duke of Hereford [later Henry IV], who was descended from John of Gaunt, the fourth son of

Edward III. Although Drayton begins the epistles after Richard's deposition, the deposition is discussed.

Elizabeth I was associated with Richard II throughout her reign.[19] After Essex's military triumphs in France (1591), he was compared with Henry V, the hero of the Battle of Agincourt. In 1594 Robert Parsons not only dedicated his *A Conference about the Next Succession* to Essex, but also stated that "no man is in more high . . . place or dignitie . . . or high liking of the people, & consequently no man like to have a greater part or sway in deciding of this great affaire . . . than your honour, and those that . . . are likest to follow your fame and fortune" (A3r). William Camden, the most reliable of English Renaissance historians, commented that after English Catholics became convinced of James's commitment to Protestantism, they even began to consider Essex as Elizabeth's successor: "they cast their eyes upon the Earle of *Essex,* (who never approved the putting men to death in the cause of Religion), feigning a Title from *Thomas of Woodstock,* King *Edward* the third's sonne, from whom he derived his Pedigree."[20] On 5 November 1595 Rowland Whyte commented that it was thought treasonous to have a copy of Parsons's book.[21] It was in this political climate that Drayton published the exchange of letters between Isabel and Richard II.

Drayton dedicated the Richard II epistles to Lucy's husband, Edward Russell, Earl of Bedford, emphasizing his eagerness to become Bedford's client: "Vouchsafe then my deare Lord to accept this *Epistle,* which I dedicate as zealously, as (I hope) you will patronize willingly, untill some more acceptable service may be witnes of my love towards your honour" (Tillotson, 112). Drayton's preface had plainly stated that he had "sorted the complection of the Epistles, to the character of theyr judgments to whom I dedicate them" (Tillotson, 101). He had associated Bedford, a prominent member of the Essex faction, with a poem about the deposition of a monarch. Since Bedford later joined the Essex rebellion, the embarrassment of the dedication only increased.

The following analysis of the Richard II epistles concentrates on those passages that appeared in the 1597 version, but were later deleted. Isabel's epistle poignantly chronicles Richard's change in fortunes:

> Thou went'st victorious, crown'd, in triumph borne,
> But cam'st subdu'd, uncrown'd, and laugh'd to scorne;
> And all those tongues which tit'led thee theyr Lord,
> Grace *Henries* glorious stile with that great word.
>
> (Tillotson, 112)

This passage was problematical because it depicted the monarch as "uncrown'd, and laugh'd to scorne." In an annotation that was later deleted Drayton tells us that Richard "confessed himselfe to be unable to governe, denounced all kingly dignitie; so that he might onely have his life" (Tillotson, 115). In actuality, Richard hoped to be remembered positively because of his willingness to abdicate and preserve the peace.

As though he has taken a leaf from Parsons's book, Drayton's Richard acknowledges that deposition is a just punishment for his sins. It is well to keep in mind that the deposition scene in Shakespeare's *Richard II* was never printed during Elizabeth's lifetime:[22]

> But justice is the heavens, the fault is mine.
> Kings pallaces stand open to let in,
> The soothing Traytor, and the guide to sin,
> Many we have in tryumphs to attend us,
> But few are left in perrill to defend us;
> Amongst the most, the worst we best can chuse.
> (Tillotson, 115)

Drayton blames self-interested councillors for Richard's deposition. He was governed by disloyal and cowardly upstarts, just as Elizabeth was being unduly influenced by the Cecils.

Drayton somewhat improbably attributes to Richard an admiring description of Henry Bullingbrook's popularity with the common people. He does not suggest, as Shakespeare does in his *I Henry IV,* that Henry is being Machiavellian:

> When *Herford* had his judgement of exile,
> Saw I the peoples murmuring the while,
> Saw I the love, the zeale, the fayth, the care,
> The Commons still to pleasing *Herford* bare;
> Fond women, and scarce-speaking children mourne,
> Weeping his parting, wishing his returne.
> (Tillotson, 115)

Essex had a similar effect on the people, although some of his contemporaries viewed his behavior more critically than Drayton did.

The portrait of Foelix in Everard Guilpin's *Skialetheia,* Satire 1, is directed at Essex:

For when great *Foelix* passing through the street,
Vayleth his cap to each one he doth meet,
And when no broome-man that will pray for him,
Shall have lesse truage then his bonnets brim,
Who would not thinke him perfect curtesie?

(63–67)[23]

Guilpin describes Essex's "yeastie ambition" and charges that Machiavelli taught him "this mumming trick" of using "curtesie / T'entrench himselfe in popularitie" (72–74).

The single most damning reference in the Richard II epistles occurs when Drayton has Richard describe his lusty ancestors and then emphasize his own "fruitlessness":

But I his graft and barraine trunke am growne
And for a fruitlesse water-bough am hewne.

(Tillotson, 114)

When Sir Edward Coke examined Sir John Hayward's *The First Part of the Life and raigne of King Henrie the IIII* (entered in the Stationers' Register 9 January 1599) for treasonous material, he concluded that references to Richard's childlessness were evidence.[24] Those who supported Richard's deposition had argued that in forcing him to abdicate, no rightful heirs would be disinherited. No matter how far-fetched parallels between the reigns of Richard II and Elizabeth may seem, on this one point there were grounds for comparison.

Fifth Set: Queen Katherine and Owen Tudor

Queen Katherine, the dowager Queen of England, was the daughter of Charles of France, the widow of Henry V (1413–22), and the mother of Henry VI (1422–61; 1470–71). After defeating Charles, Henry V married Charles's daughter Katherine in 1420 and was acknowledged as heir to France, but died in 1422. His son Henry VI was officially crowned in 1429 as the King of France and England. In 1427 an act was passed forbidding the dowager queen to remarry without the king's permission. Her secret marriage to Owen Tudor is assumed to have taken place in 1429. Drayton's epistles are exchanged just before the marriage.

Drayton's portraits of Katherine and Owen Tudor have plausibility and charm. The Dowager Queen Katherine mocks the notion that the Lancastrians are gods like Apollo and Diana while all others are the "Brats of wofull *Niobe*" (70). She defiantly observes that she is a princess of France and that Owen Tudor is descended from Welsh kings, warriors who frequently defeated the English in battle. Drayton's Katherine is the fully realized daughter, wife, and mother of kings. Confident in her own lineage, she wittily uses mythological allusions to ridicule the pride of the Lancastrians.

Drayton's Katherine probably would have worried about lineage when attracted to Owen Tudor and might have raised that issue in a letter written to the commoner who was her lover. This focus on lineage, though probable from a literary or historical perspective, was not politically astute. The Tudor claim to the throne of England was not based on descent from Welsh kings, although Henry VII invented a royal Welsh background. Katherine jeers at the lineage of Henry V, who descended from John of Gaunt, the fourth son of Edward III, but Henry Tudor traced his descent from the same John of Gaunt except through the illegitimate Beaufort line. By having Katherine concentrate on lineage, Drayton needlessly draws attention to the issue of bloodlines. Those alert to genealogy, that is the majority of English nobility, were aware of claims among the old nobility as well as the approaching end of the Tudor line.

Owen Tudor reminds Katherine that Merlin prophesied that "Kings and Queenes" would "follow in the Tudor line" (36), but Drayton is more interested in characterization than politics. There are flashes of humor in Owen Tudor's epistle that play upon Shakespeare's characterization of the Welsh Owen Glendower in *I Henry IV*. In act 2 Glendower regales Hotspur with a description of the omens that marked his birth:

> . . . Give me leave
> To tell you once again that at my birth
> The front of heaven was full of fiery shapes,
> The goats ran from the mountains, and the herds
> Were strangely clamorous to the frighted fields.
> (2.1.35–39)

In contrast to Shakespeare's imaginative and boastful Owen Glendower, Drayton's Owen Tudor announces that he does not derive his birth from the heavens and that he does not exaggerate his deeds and talents. Drayton also alludes to the folk humor that represented the Welsh as boasters and liars. Owen Tudor comments that he, at least, does not stand "on tip-toes in Superlatives," although the English like to mock Welsh "Hyperbolies" (2.64, 66).

Sixth Set: Queen Margaret and William de la Pole

The epistles exchanged between William de la Pole, Duke of Suffolk, and Queen Margaret, wife of the Lancastrian Henry VI, focus directly on the political maneuvering that immediately preceded the War of the Roses. At his death Henry V appointed his brother Humphrey, Duke of Gloucester, regent during the minority of his son, Henry VI (1422–61; 1470–71). Suffolk promoted the marriage of Margaret, daughter of the Duke of Anjou, to Henry VI in 1445. To gain Margaret for Henry VI, Suffolk agreed that England would cede Anjou, Mans, and Maine to her father. In 1450 Suffolk was accused of the murder of Duke Humphrey (1447) and of engineering England's loss of Normandy. As a punishment, Suffolk was sentenced to exile for five years; he writes his letter in 1450 before he sets sail for France.

Even though these epistles had less immediate political significance for events in 1597 than the reigns of Edward II and Richard II, it was still problematic to write an unbiased account of the War of the Roses, if only because the old nobility were engaged on one side or another. Drayton recognized this difficulty, and he resolved it by using his historical notes to comment ironically upon the epistles of Margaret and William, Duke of Suffolk. These epistles represent Drayton's most successful integration of fiction and fact.

Suffolk claims that the Nevilles arranged his exile to get him out of the way so that they could supplant the Lancastrian Henry VI with the York claimant. Warwick, according to Suffolk, has kindled a "long hidden fire" in "Yorkes stern Brest" (40). Suffolk sneeringly dismisses the charge that he murdered Humphrey, Duke of Gloucester:

> . . . since the old decrepit Duke is dead,
> By me, of force, he must be murthered.
> If they would know who rob'd him of his Life,
> Let him call home *Dame Elinor,* his Wife.
> (47–50)

Drayton's note corrects Suffolk's claim that his exile resulted from charges trumped up by Warwick: "*Humphrey,* Duke of *Gloucester,* and Lord Protector, . . . by the meanes of the *Queene,* and the Duke of *Suffolke,* was arrested . . . and the same Night after murthered in his Bed" (2:236).

Throughout the epistles of Suffolk and Margaret, Drayton allows them to present their evidence convincingly. Neither Suffolk nor Margaret experiences qualms about vilifying Warwick or the Yorks. There is no hint of irony until their epistles are juxtaposed with the notes.

We might expect Drayton to evade the issue of who had the better claim to the throne, the Lancasters or the Yorks. Suffolk claims that Warwick has used York's lineage as a pretext in order to put his own pawn on the throne:

> By *Clarence* Title working to supplant
> The Eagle-Ayrie of great *John* of *Gaunt*.
> (41–42)

The note to this passage unequivocally states that the York claim was superior: "to whom the Crowne, after King *Richard* the Seconds Death, lineally descended, he dying without Issue; and not to the Heires of the Duke of *Lancaster,* that was younger Brother to the Duke of *Clarence*. Hall.cap. I. Tit. Yor. & Lanc." (2:236). The sources for most of the notes are not given, but Drayton cites Hall and supplies a more explicit citation than usual on this touchy issue.

Drayton's Suffolk resembles Marlowe's "overreachers"; his aspiring mind cannot be constrained: "Our Faulcons kind cannot the Cage indure" (17). Undaunted by his exile, Suffolk remains stoic about what the future holds because fortune cannot shake a "true-resolved Mind":

> Man in himself a little World doth beare,
> His Soule the Monarch, ever ruling there:
> Where-ever then his Body doth remaine,
> He is a King, that in himselfe doth raigne.
> (25–28)

Suffolk simply but powerfully delivers the Renaissance commonplace that self-rule enables a man to withstand adversity.

Drayton's Margaret is not, like Shakespeare's, a "tiger's heart wrapped in a woman's hide," although she, too, curses the Yorks with resounding spleen. She despises her husband Henry, who while others "raze the Crowne from of his head . . . (like a woman) sits him downe to weepe" (Tillotson, 125). In lines that are later cut Drayton unwisely allows her contempt to lead her to question Henry's legitimacy:

> Nor can he come from *Lancasters* great line,
> Or from the wombe of beautious *Katherine*.
> (Tillotson, 125)

It was impolitic to raise the issue of legitimacy in regard to English sovereigns. English Catholics regarded Elizabeth as illegitimate because they did not recognize Henry VIII's divorce. The problem of her legitimacy was exacerbated because her mother had been executed for adultery. James's paternity was also questioned because Mary, Queen of Scots, was rumored to have committed adultery.

Drayton attributes Suffolk's attraction to Margaret to a magnetism between powerful spirits. In his epistle Suffolk describes the sumptuousness of the marriage he arranged in her honor and then asks:

> Judge if his kindnesse have not power to move,
> Who for his loves sake gave away his love.
>
> (111–12)

Margaret regards Suffolk as godlike in his charms; Jove, she says, could have been more successful in his amorous exploits if he had adopted Suffolk's shape. She is tormented because she fears for Suffolk's safety, and in a dream, like that of Hero in Ovid's *Heroides,* she foresees his death at sea.

She also voices fears that dominated late sixteenth-century military policy: fear of popular rebellion, concern about invasion from either Scotland or Ireland, and the threat of a standing army, susceptible to control by faction. These fears influenced Elizabeth's reaction to Essex's unauthorized return from Ireland in 1599. Drayton's Margaret voices these fears in terms of Jack Cades's rebellion, but the rebellion actually occurred after Suffolk's death. Margaret fears York because he has returned from Ireland with forces that enable him to seize the throne. Concerned about Suffolk's safety, Margaret concludes her epistle because her tears are falling so rapidly that they blot her lines.

In these epistles Drayton movingly portrays two figures against the historical background of a complex struggle for power. That the issue of lineage, a crucial political issue in the War of the Roses, is handled in notes to these epistles defines Drayton's point of view. He does not depict Providence working in English history to bring about the entrance of the Tudors in large part because he is interested in individual historical figures. The rightness or the wrongness of the cause is relegated to the background; focus is on the character of Suffolk "who for his loves sake gave away his love" (112).

Seventh Set: King Edward IV and Mistress Jane Shore

With the assistance of Warwick, the "Kingmaker," the historical Edward IV (1461–83) deposes Henry VI in 1461, but Drayton's epistles portray him as the wooer of Jane Shore in 1470, not as a soldier. As in the previous epistle, the notes are used as historical counterpoint to Drayton's literary portrait; his notes denigrate Edward as effectively as Margaret ridicules the effete Henry VI. Drayton first remarks that since the Edward-Jane epistles concern "unlawfull Affection," he has included few historical notes. Since four of the preceding epistles also concerned adulterous passion, this explanation is unconvincing. In part, Drayton recognized that the intrusion of Edward's public career would violate the decorum of these epistles: "for had he mentioned the many Battels betwixt the *Lancastrian* Faction and him, or other Warlike Dangers, it had beene more like to Plautus boasting Souldier, then a Kingly Courtier" (2:252). Edward would indeed appear to be a braggart soldier if he brought up his military prowess in the midst of his seduction attempt. Drayton, however, does not depict Edward as a "Kingly Courtier"; Edward has willfully allowed his sensuality to dominate his character. Throughout his letter to Jane Shore Edward uses his "kingly" status as a ploy to enhance his chances of succeeding at seduction: no recollection of Jane Shore's duty to her husband should be allowed to "countermaund a Monarchs high desire" (5).

In contrast to Henry II whose love for Rosamond was sincere, Edward appears incapable of "amorous affection." Edward woos Jane Shore with two temptations: a more exalted social position in the court and sensual treats. He describes her beauty lying in a "meane" bed, "like an un-cut Diamond in Lead" (27–28). Cunningly he offers to adorn her with a "Kingly State" (24), claiming figuratively that the beauty of her stone is spoiled "[w]anting the gracious Ornament of Gilt" (32). The use of images of jewels and gold is thematically appropriate because Jane Shore's husband is a jeweler, but Edward's repeated comparison of Jane with rich jewels and constant references to buying and selling suggest that Jane can be bought and Edward can pay the price.

The historical notes emphasize Edward's public career as a monarch. With heavy irony, Drayton observes: "And albeit Princes, whilest they live, have nothing in them but what is admirable; yet we need not mistrust the flatterie of the Court in those Times: For certaine it is, that his shape was excellent" (2:252). After conceding the physical attractions of Edward IV, Drayton proceeds in the note to use his features as evidence that Edward had "much sharpenesse of Understanding, and Crueltie, mingled together" and an "affection of Tyrannie" (252). Although Drayton nods at the moral disapproval

typical of the Mirror tradition, his point of view is astonishingly liberated.
Edward is one of those who "rather leave their Children what to possesse,
then what to imitate" (252). Drayton is disturbed by Edward's valueless ma-
terialism, more than by his sexual immorality. His portrait of Edward reflects
this judgment.

Edward, unlike the gay seducers who woo their mistresses by reminding
them that time will take away their charms, uses his kingship as a rich bait.
He pictures Jane Shore in "a Princes sumptuous Gallerie":

> . . . and from thy State shalt see
> The Tilts and Triumphs that are done for thee.
> Then know the diff'rence (if thou list to prove)
> Betwixt a Vulgar and a Kingly love.
>   (156–60)

Telling Jane that it is not cunning to be coy, Edward concludes with a veiled
threat: "Whilst lazie Time his turne by tarriance serves, / Love still growes
sickly" (165–66). Edward is cunning enough to hint that his attraction to
Jane may not last.

In her epistle Jane Shore seems to have acquiesced already in her seduction,
but she feels none of Rosamond's remorse. She echoes appreciatively the various ploys that Edward has offered her, acknowledging that "Fame must attend on that, which lives in Court" (22):

> What Swan of bright *Apollo's* Brood doth sing,
> To vulgar Love, in Courtly Soneting?
> Or what immortall Poets sugred Pen
> Attends the glory of a Citizen?
>   (23–26)

Jane Shore's conviction that "Apollo's Brood" will not sing "courtly" sonnets
about a mere citizen is rendered ironic because Drayton is only superficially
proving her point. With his "sugred Pen" he is describing her love, but it is a
"vulgar Love." Coy and light-minded, Jane first pleads the weakness of a
woman faced with the wiles of a male seducer, then acknowledges that a husband may get accustomed to his wife and cease to be as bold and expert at
sporting "with *Venus* in a Bed of Downe" (128). Her vulgarity is confirmed
when she acknowledges that she might be able to resist "meaner men," but
"when Kings once come, they conquer as they list" (160).

Eighth Set: Mary Tudor, Queen of France, and Charles Brandon

After epistles on the War of the Roses we might expect Drayton to offer epistles exchanged between Henry Tudor, the red rose, and Elizabeth of York, the white rose, and so to celebrate the Tudor myth, but instead he turns in his eighth set of epistles to a couple whose descendants in 1597 complicated the Elizabethan succession question. Henry VIII (1509–47) married his younger sister, Mary Tudor, to Louis, the aging King of France, in October 1514. According to Drayton's version of their romance, when Louis died in January 1515, Charles Brandon, later Duke of Suffolk, was sent to bring Mary back to England; he married her in 1515. Mary writes her epistle before their marriage because Brandon has been delayed.

Had Drayton portrayed them positively, his selection of this particular couple would be easier to understand, but his Mary Tudor is surprisingly worldly. Questioning why Brandon has not yet arrived in France, she compares their relationship to that of Hero and Leander, observing that even though Leander had the Hellespont to swim, that arduous task did not prevent him from coming to Hero. She adds that there is no nurse to chide or leer at them if "wantoning, [they] revell in [her] Towre" (16).

Mary is frank about her sexuality, more so than any female figure in the epistles except Jane Shore. Although in love with Brandon, her attitudes toward sex and marriage are pragmatic. Acknowledging that her marriage was consummated, she counters her revelation with careless ambition:

> For Maydenhead, he on my Head set a Crowne.
> Who would not change a Kingdome for a Kisse?
> (118–19)

Mary's witty play on "Maydenhead" and her crowned head is then shrugged off as a "Kingdome for a Kisse." She offers a list of the men she might marry, but then prefers Brandon's charm and "the shape thou art adorn'd withall" (168).

Drayton's Mary concludes her epistle coyly. If her brother objects to their love, she brags that she will deceive him by saying that she only "fancied" Brandon "to frame my liking to his mind" (179, 181). In a passage later deleted she adds (183–84):

Should not the sister like as doth the Brother,
The one of us should be unlike the other.
(Tillotson, 129)

Drayton's Mary is as impolitic as her creator. After asking a question that recalls Henry VIII's colorful marital career, she laughingly dismisses the objec-
tions of the "idle Commons" who will want her to marry a "Yorkist,"
"Lancastrian," or into the "Line of great Plantaginet" (184–88). If Mary appeared to be overwhelmed by passionate love, her cavalier attitude toward
England's future might be less disturbing.

In his epistle Brandon, somewhat perversely, imagines Louis weak and
crippled in bed, desiring Mary, but not able to take full advantage of her
beauty: "to be of all beguil'd / And yet still longing like a little Child" (107–
8). With practiced flattery, he attributes his prowess at her wedding jousts to
the inspiration of a tiny tear in her eyes. In a calculating manner he concludes
his letter by assuring Mary of the loyalty of his ancestors to the Tudors. He is
already developing strategies to justify their marriage to Henry.

The descendants of Mary Tudor and Charles Brandon had a strong claim
to the succession. When Henry VIII had Parliament formally determine
the succession, he designated his children, Edward, Mary, and Elizabeth,
but then altered the natural order from the heirs of his older sister, Margaret
of Scotland, to the heirs of his younger sister, Mary (Tudor) Brandon,
Duchess of Suffolk. The family names become complicated because
Mary's union with Suffolk produced daughters and granddaughters,
whose family names changed to Grey (Dorset title) and Seymour (Hertford
title) when they married.

Ninth Set: Guilford Dudley and Lady Jane Grey

When Edward VI (1547–53), the son and heir of Henry VIII, became
seriously ill, John Dudley, Duke of Northumberland, arranged for his fourth
son Guilford Dudley to marry Lady Jane Grey on 21 May 1553. Jane was
the eldest daughter of Frances Brandon, the descendant of Mary Tudor and
Charles Brandon. Thus, Drayton's ninth and last set of epistles concerns the
fate of Jane Grey, the eldest granddaughter of Mary (Tudor) Brandon of the
previous epistles. Lady Jane Grey was proclaimed queen after Edward's
death, but the people rose in support of Mary Tudor, daughter of Henry
VIII. The epistles of Lady Jane and Guilford Dudley are written just before
their executions in 1554. This grim conclusion to *Englands Heroicall Epistles*

was especially tactless on Drayton's part because there was a living Suffolk claimant.

After Jane's execution, her sister, Catherine Grey became the next Suffolk claimant. She was married first to the son of the Earl of Pembroke, who repudiated the marriage after Mary's accession. She next married Edward Seymour, Earl of Hertford. By act of Parliament it was illegal for anyone with a claim to the throne to marry without Elizabeth's consent. Elizabeth refused to acknowledge the legality of the Grey-Seymour marriage and imprisoned Catherine for the rest of her life. After Catherine died, the doubtful blessing of the Suffolk claim passed to Edward Seymour, Viscount Beauchamp, her son by the Earl of Hertford. In 1595 when Hertford was unwise enough to petition to confirm the legality of his marriage to protect the inheritance of his son, Elizabeth sent him to the Tower of London until he thought better of his request. The legitimacy of Edward Seymour, Hertford's son, was not acknowledged until 1604 after Elizabeth I's death and James's accession.

Drayton portrays Lady Jane as a Protestant martyr who, although imprisoned and about to die, retains her faith.[25] She prophesies that Elizabeth will inherit the crown from Mary and "cast aside the heavie Yoke of *Spaine*" (2.182). In lines that were later cut, Dudley replies in his epistle by praising Jane's wisdom and beauty as befitting a queen:

> Mee thinks thy wisedome was ordained alone,
> To blesse a scepter, beautifie a throne;
> Thy lyps a sacred oracle retaine,
> Wherein all holy prophecies remaine.
>
> (Tillotson, 136)

The prominence of the Suffolk claim rendered it impolitic to emphasize Jane's regal nature and praise her as blessing "a scepter" and beautifying a "throne." Guilford Dudley's epistle echoes Jane's tribute to Elizabeth, but weakly:

> And yet that heaven *Elizabeth* may blesse,
> Be thou (sweet *Jane*) a faithfull Prophitesse.
>
> (Tillotson, 136)

Drayton concludes not with a salute to Elizabeth, but with praise of Lady Jane Grey.

The epistles of Lady Jane Grey and Guilford Dudley are dedicated to Frances Goodere, whom Drayton describes as like Jane "in all perfection,

both of wisdom and learning" (Tillotson, 134). Since he concludes the last
set of epistles with a dedication stating that the characters of Frances Goodere
and Lady Jane Grey resemble each other, his insistence on this connection reinforces his prefatory statement that the dedicatees are connected with their
epistles.

Design of *Englands Heroicall Epistles*

To summarize the design of the 1597 version of this work, the third,
fourth, fifth, and sixth sets of epistles examine the reigns of three lawful
kings who were deposed, Edward II, Richard II, and Henry VI. After the
epistles related to the War of the Roses (Henry VI and Edward IV), an Elizabethan audience might expect a celebration of the Tudor union of the red
roses of Lancaster and white roses of York. Drayton, however, moves to recent history and concludes his poem with two epistles concerning the ancestors of the Suffolk claimant to the English throne. The last set of epistles
sympathetically portrays Lady Jane Grey and Guilford Dudley as martyrs.
That their letters were written just before their executions graphically fore-
shadowed the ruthless jockeying for position likely if Elizabeth died before
naming a successor.

The dedications to the two Catholic dedicatees, Lord Monteagle and Lord
Henry Howard, were removed after the 1597 edition appeared and before
1598 was printed. When these dedications were removed in 1598, Drayton
added five new epistles. Immediately preceding those concerned with the deposition of Richard II, he added amatory epistles related to Edward the Black
Prince. After the exchange between Owen Tudor and Queen Katherine, he
inserted the letters of Elinor Cobham and Duke Humphrey before those of
William de la Pole and Margaret. The Elinor Cobham epistles extend the
treatment of the War of the Roses and offer new perspectives on Suffolk and
Margaret, but their interest is psychological, not political.

In 1598 Drayton also decided to break up the eighth and ninth sets of
epistles. He inserted the romantic epistle of Henry Howard, Earl of Surrey, to
Geraldine, Elizabeth Fitzgerald (1528–89), daughter of the ninth Earl of
Kildare, between the Mary Tudor and Lady Jane Grey epistles. He dedicated
the Surrey epistle (1598) to Henry Lucas. Inclusion of the Surrey epistle violates Drayton's overall design of writing about English monarchs. He may
have hoped to make the epistles less susceptible to political interpretation by
introducing the Surrey epistle between the Brandon and Grey epistles, but
his violaton of the design calls attention to the revision.

Since Drayton left the epistles in chronological order and still concluded with the Lady Jane Grey and Guilford Dudley epistles, the political thrust of *Englands Heroicall Epistles* was less obvious after the additions, but it had not disappeared, as the following list illustrates.

1597	1)	Rosamond and King Henry II.
1597	2)	King John and Matilda; Monteagle dedication deleted before 1598.
1597	3)	Queen Isabel and Mortimer.
1598		*Edward the Black Prince and Alice, Countess of Salisbury (two epistles); no dedication until 1602 and then dedicated to Sir Walter Aston.*
1597	4)	Queen Isabel and Richard II.
1597	5)	Queen Katherine and Owen Tudor; Howard dedication deleted before 1598.
1598		*Elinor Cobham and Duke Humphrey (two epistles), with new dedication to James Huish.*
1597	6)	Queen Margaret and William de la Pole.
1597	7)	Edward IV and Mistress Jane Shore.
1597	8)	Mary Tudor, Queen of France, and Charles Brandon.
1598		*Henry Howard, Earl of Surrey, to Lady Geraldine (one epistle), with new dedication to Henry Lucas.*
1597	9)	Guilford Dudley and Lady Jane Grey.

Judging from the tone of the new dedications to Henry Lucas and James Huish, added respectively in 1598 and 1599, Drayton assumed snobbery, not politics, had motivated the withdrawal of dedications by the two Catholic noblemen, Monteagle and Howard.

In July 1598 Essex had quarreled with Elizabeth over who should be charged with bringing Ireland to heel, provoking her so much that she boxed his ears in a council meeting. He halfway drew his sword and stormed away from the court.[26] Drayton either ignored or failed to understand the political storm that was brewing in 1598. He neither removed nor revised allusions that might be construed as comments on Essex or the Cecils, and he did not change the dedication of the Richard II epistles to the Earl of Bedford.

Of the material added in 1598, the epistle of Henry Howard, Earl of Surrey, offers the most insight into Drayton's revisions. Drawing upon Thomas Nashe's *The Unfortunate Traveller* (1594), he describes Surrey as writing from Italy to Geraldine. Two themes are emphasized: 1) the English language and 2) the function of the poet. After apologizing for writing in English while so near the "Muses sacred Spring" in Tuscany (2.8), Surrey concedes that Italian may be smoother, but insists:

> Our Dialect no Majestie doth want,
> To set thy praises in as high a Key,
> As *France,* or *Spaine,* or *Germanie.*
>
> (2:12–14)

The poet replaces the military leader as hero. Surrey describes himself as one of "*Apollo's* Heires" and observes that even princes sing his lines. When Heaven strives to do the most that it can, it spends its "utmost pow'r," creating a poet (113–15).

> That little diff'rence 'twixt the Gods and us,
> (By them confirm'd) distinguish'd onely thus:
> Whom they, in Birth, ordaine to happy dayes,
> The Gods commit their glory to our prayse.
>
> (17–20)

Poets praise those ordained for "happy days"; references to heroic valor are noticeably absent. A poet can also preserve his mistress's charms: Surrey's verses can give Geraldine back her golden hair when her locks have turned to gray. This epistle accentuates romantic elements in *Englands Heroicall Epistles,* offering an implicit defense of the epistles as poetic fictions—the work of a poet who was immortalizing English lovers.

Although it was decided that Essex would go to Ireland by November 1598, English forces did not cross the Irish Sea until April 1599. In January 1599 Sir John Hayward printed his *First Part of the Life and Raigne of King Henrie the IIII* warmly dedicated to the Earl of Essex.[27] Hayward's history of Henry IV did not immediately get him in trouble, but by 1 March 1599 John Chamberlain was writing about Hayward's history to Dudley Carlton: "Here hath ben much descanting about it why such a storie shold come out at this time, and many exceptions taken, especially to the epistle which was a short thinge in Latin dedicated to the erle of Essex."[28] On 1 June 1599 a number of works were burned by order of the Archbishop of Canterbury and the Bishop of London. The printing of any English history was forbidden unless it was authorized by a member of the Privy Council.[29]

On 26 September 1599 in defiance of Elizabeth's orders, Essex returned from Ireland with a few retainers and forced his way into the queen's bed-chamber. He was banished from the court and put into the custody of Sir Thomas Egerton. Apparently convinced that Essex's fortunes would turn around, Drayton prepared a new edition but deleted no allusions to Essex. In 1599 he removed the reference to Richard II as a "barraine trunk."[30] He also appended a selection of twenty-one sonnets from *Ideas Mirrour* (1594), as well as nineteen new sonnets, and a new epistle, Geraldine's reply to Surrey.

Geraldine is one of Drayton's most charming and successful literary creations, but in spite of the strife between England and Ireland in 1599, he makes her an Irish patriot. Denying that her house derives from Italy, she claims "greater worth unto my Bloud" is given by "*Irish* Milke" (73–74) and boasts of the pure air of her homeland. Since English troops had embarked for Ireland the previous April to put down rebellion, Geraldine's Irish patriotism is problematical. Because Drayton relies on his annotations to interpret the argument of his epistles, the reader has been alerted to pay attention to them. In the notes to the Geraldine epistle he states that Robert, Earl of Essex, is a descendant of Geraldine. This allusion, presumably a compliment to Essex, associates *Englands Heroicall Epistles* (1599) with Essex's abortive Irish campaign.

Geraldine's epistle was the last to be added to *Englands Heroicall Epistles*, bringing the total number of epistles to twenty-four in 1599. Drayton ends her epistle on a far from positive note. Geraldine observes that poets are not rewarded by courtly patrons:

> Few live in Court that of their good have care,
> The *Muses* friends are every-where so rare.
> (143–44)

Geraldine also criticizes the impact of the court on poetry, a theme that dominates Drayton's Jacobean and Caroline verse:

> [t]he Noblest Spirits to Vertue most inclin'd,
> These here in Court thy greatest want doe find.
> (175–76)

By 1599, Drayton must have realized that contemporary events were making his epistles increasingly susceptible to political interpretation. He supplies a graceful literary conclusion to the Geraldine epistle. Echoing the opening line of Ovid's *Heroides,* Geraldine concludes:

> Then, as Ulysses Wife, write I to thee,
> Make no reply, but come thy selfe to mee.
>   (181–82)

The literary flavor of Geraldine's Ovidian allusion did not offset Drayton's celebration of her Irish patriotism and her kinship with Essex.

Essex was released from Egerton's custody in March 1600 and allowed to return to Essex house. By February 1600 Sir John Hayward was under investigation by the Star Chamber. The notes of Attorney General Edward Coke accuse Hayward of selecting a story "200 years old . . . intending the application of it to this time, the plot being that of a King who is taxed for misgovernment and his council for corrupt and covetous dealings for private ends."[31] Unlike John Chamberlain, who found "no such buggeswords" (bogies, imaginary fears) or Francis Bacon, who found only plagiarism from Tacitus in Hayward's history, Coke found treason.[32]

By 1600 Drayton recognized that Essex was unlikely to regain favor. He excised brief passages from the Isabel and Mortimer epistles (Edward II), toned down the positive treatment of Lady Jane Grey and Guilford Dudley, but engaged in a wholesale revision of the Richard II epistles. Since Drayton was able to make substantial changes in the Richard II epistle, he presumably could have removed the dedication of that epistle to the Earl of Bedford, but he left it untouched.

Hayward was committed to the Tower in July 1600, more than six months before the Essex rebellion occurred on 8 February 1601, and remained in the Tower until James arrived in London. In the instructions to preachers regarding the Essex rebellion prepared by the Privy Council, Hayward's book is described as "cunningly insinuating that the same abuses being now in this realm that were in the days of Richard II, the like course might be taken for redress."[33] Although the Privy Council records for this period were destroyed in a seventeenth-century fire, much of the material has been reconstructed. Drayton's *Englands Heroicall Epistles* appears not to have received the close reading and political interpretation given to Hayward's history of Henry IV.

The course of history itself, however, was to make *Englands Heroicall Epistles* increasingly awkward for Drayton's patrons. The Earl of Bedford participated in the Essex rebellion and was fined twenty thousand pounds. The fine was later reduced to ten thousand, but much of the Bedford estate was entailed for the next heir and his fine exceeded Lucy's handsome dowry of three thousand pounds. Drayton was fortunate that the more politically volatile first edition of *Englands Heroicall Epistles* appeared in 1597, rather than

1599, or he might well have kept Hayward company in the Tower. The timing was still unfortunate for a work designed to attract patronage. When contemporary events began to turn his historical poem into increasingly disturbing political commentary, Drayton reacted by changing too little too late.

Chapter Four

Patronage and Poetry: 1600–1607

Drayton's laureate aspirations, and his dependence upon patronage for recognition, continued to influence his poetry after James's accession. His conception of the poet as a guardian of heroic values and a spokesman for virtue, unmistakably diverged from those of Jacobean patrons who expected poets to compose witty compliments and clever entertainments for court ceremonies. From 1600 through 1606 Drayton tried to strike a balance between taking risks and lapsing into obsequious flattery. The tensions reflected in his work during this period illuminate the complexity of the patronage system. He aspired to recognition, but not if too many concessions were required, and he became increasingly intolerant of patronage conventions. In his early seventeenth-century poetry Drayton wavers between accommodation and assertion until he finally commits himself and spurns court patronage, symbolically rejecting the system of literary clientage.

In 1600 Drayton published a sonnet addressed to James VI of Scotland with *Englands Heroicall Epistles* in the latest version of *Idea*. His compliment to James suggests that he realized that James's succession was more likely than that of any of his competitors. Although presumably intended as a gesture of accommodation, Drayton's praise of James in 1600 was not well-timed. Lord Henry Howard, who may have asked to have the dedication addressed to him withdrawn from *Englands Heroicall Epistles*, was already in close contact with James. Sir Robert Cecil was to begin a secret correspondence with James shortly after the Essex rebellion in 1601. Even so, most literary men cautiously postponed their tributes to James until after his accession. While in the Tower Sir John Hayward prepared *An Answer to the First Part of a certaine Conference, concerning Succession, published not long since under the name of R. Doleman* (1603). Only after James's accession did he publish his "defense of succession according to proximitie of bloud" with a dedication to James, affirming that his current tract and his earlier history of Henry IV "were undertaken with particular respect, to your Majesties just title of succession."[1]

Drayton's premature dedication of a sonnet to James again illustrates his lack of prudence. He concludes his sonnet with a plea to James to support and promote poets who immortalize the names of kings:

> That they whose pens, (even) life to Kings doe give,
> In thee a King, shall seeke them selves to live.
>   (1:488.13–15)

Drayton expected great things from James, but his expectations were not to be fulfilled.

The Barons Warres

The Barons Warres (1603), a poem of six cantos, more than 3,600 lines in ottava rima, returns to the subject of Edward II and his struggles with the barons led by Roger Mortimer and Queen Isabel. As his new title suggests, war becomes a more important theme in *The Barons Warres* than it had been in *Mortimeriados* or *Peirs Gaveston*. Drayton's dedication to Sir Walter Aston differs from his earlier effusive dedications to Lucy in 1594, 1595, 1596, and 1597. He tells Aston that as a client he will not follow the "formall ordinary course" that others "vulgarly faine" (2:381.3–4).[2] He describes their clientage relationship as founded on "firme and true election" (6) and asserts his personal independence:

> Nor walke more publicke, nor obscurer wayes,
> Then Vertue bids, and Judgement will allow.
>   (11–12)

Drayton's "self-fashioned role" identifies him as an independent client willing to serve a patron who shares his regard for virtue.[3]

The "judgment," alluded to in Drayton's dedication to Aston, is reflected in the tone of *The Barons Warres*. His treatment of the wars between Edward II and the barons shows that he recognized the political risk of writing about deposed monarchs; sections of *The Barons Warres* become orations illustrating the evils of civil discord. Between the appearance of *Mortimeriados* in 1596 and *The Barons Warres* seven years later in 1603, Drayton also refined his conception of heroic verse. He moved away from the rhetorical exuberance of his earlier historical poetry toward a Jacobean style, in which narrative structure controls the apostrophes and scene painting. In *The Barons Warres* he includes apostrophes to Providence and Fate, a heroic catalog of warriors

by shire (canto 1), a seven-line allegory on Mischief (canto 2), and epic ma-
chinery to suggest the change from day to night.

These stylistic changes accompany an increased literary dependence on the
Latin poet Lucan and Samuel Daniel's *Civile Wars* (1595 and 1599 five
books, 1601 six books, 1609 eight books). Lucan was studied in Elizabethan grammar schools, and his *Pharsalia* figured as an appropriate model for
the historical epic. In spite of Francis Meres's willingness to find a profuse
number of English counterparts for every classical author, he compares only
Spenser and Warner with Homer and Vergil; Daniel and Drayton become
English Lucans (74).[4] Typically, Lucan favors orations, apostrophes, and
elaborate scene painting; nearly one-third of his *Pharsalia* consists of rhetorical set speeches. Daniel, like Lucan, frequently uses extended similes, some of
which are borrowed from the *Pharsalia,* but Daniel differs from Lucan by
paying scrupulous attention to facts and ignoring personalities. Although he
condemns those who cause the civil war, Daniel avoids portraying the rebels
as villains before they rebel. Lucan exploits every opportunity to vilify the
Julian line. Unlike Daniel, Drayton is interested in personalities rather than
the sweep of history, but he tries to be unbiased.[5]

Like both Lucan and Daniel, Drayton repudiates factions that erupt into
civil discord. From the outset he takes the position that the barons were not
justified in opposing their "naturall Soveraigne":

> The bloudie Factions and Rebellious pride
> Of a strong Nation, whose ill-managed might
> Them from their naturall Soveraigne did divide,
> Their due subjection, and his lawfull right,
> Whom their light error loosely doth misguide,
> Urg'd by lewd Minions tyrannous despight.
> (Tillotson, 1.1–6)

Even though the "lawfull right" of the "naturall Soveraigne" is acknowledged, Drayton still suggests that the king's favorites, his "lewd Minions,"
are tyrannical, even if the king is not. Drayton's epic question: "what Hellish
Furie poys'ned their hot Bloud?" (2.1) suggests that the Furies, metaphysical
forces beyond human control, have caused the civil war.

Drayton carefully avoids suggesting approval of the deposition of a king
by stressing the sanctity of royal blood and the honor due the crown. Through
their "strange Conspiracies" (Tillotson, 9.70), the barons engage in "innat-
ural wrongs unto their naturall King" (Tillotson, 9.72). In canto 5, stanza 9,
Drayton discards his persona, interrupting the narrative to cut short the

Bishop of Hereford's impeachment speech. The poet warns his muse that justification for the deposition of a king must not be given at length:

> Pardon me art, that striving to be short,
> To this intent a Speech delivering;
> And that at full I doe not heare report
> Matters that tuch deposing of the King.
> (Tillotson, 9.65–68)

Somewhat artifically, he warns his muse not to "report that reasons forcibly were laid" to this "abhored thing" (9.10). In *Mortimeriados* Edward's speech to his murderers emphasizes his misery:

> I am a King, though King of miserie,
> I am your King, though wanting Majestie.
> (2,034–35)

In *The Barons Warres,* canto 5, Edward tells his murderers that "fame even hoarce with age your shame shall ring . . . by recounting of so vile a fact" (Tillotson, 62.492–93); criminals will "count their Wickedness scarce sinne, / To that which long before their time hath beene" (Tillotson, 62.495–96). In 1603 the outrage of killing a king far outweighs Edward's failings.

In spite of Drayton's acceptance of the sanctity of kingship and "natural sovereignty," he does not vilify Edward's enemies, Mortimer and Isabel. He introduces Mortimer in canto 1 as a great-souled hero, "compact of cleere ascending fire," whose nobility and virtue "shew'd that his pitch was boundless as the sky" (Tillotson, 21.166, 176). When the young and beautiful Isabel is introduced, we are told that she has been "basely rejected" and denied her "soveraigne state" (Tillotson, 30.233–34). Also, in canto 1 the barons feel that their ancient "Privilege" of "Free-birth" (25.193) has been undermined by "lascivious Minion[s]" who "tryumphing boast" of their humiliation (25.195; Tillotson, 197). Drayton attempts to do justice to the noble Mortimer, the injured Isabel, and the aggrieved barons while upholding Edward II's sanctity as sovereign.

Although *The Barons Warres,* examined by itself, appears politic enough, Drayton's refusal to take sides renders this poem subversive, if its tone is compared with a contemporary treatment of Edward II. Richard Niccols added a version of the fall of Edward II to his revised edition of *A Mirrour for Magistrates* (1610).[6] Niccols has no difficulty in identifying the villians and differentiating them from the party of the rightful king. Isabel secures Mortimer's release from prison to "coole her lust burnt blood with dregs of shame" (Aaa8). The morality is clear. We are to deplore the "incontinence" of this "disloyall Queen" (Aaa7v). Sympathy is even extended to Edward II's favorites, who are loyal servants of the monarch, not Drayton's "lascivious minions." Niccols sympathizes with a favorite that "in [the] bosome of a Prince doth dwell." A loyal servant, who dutifully obliges his monarch, will be slandered:

> Yet as the Deere pursu'd from place to place,
> The envious dog will have him still in chase.
> Danger in chiefest safetie it doth bring
> To seeme to be familiar with a king.
>
> (Aaa5)

Those "familiar with a king" will be chased by "envious" dogs. Niccols's version of Edward II illustrates how Jacobean history was supposed to be written. While willing to repudiate faction and civil discord, Drayton refuses to supply the expected political moral.

Critical opinion on *The Barons Warres* has not always agreed that it is an improvement over *Mortimeriados*. John Buxton approves of the revision, but Richard F. Hardin regards Drayton's introduction of additional historical material as "an attempt to show off his scholarship" and concludes that his shift to the ottava rima stanza results in padding.[7] This mixed evaluation underlines that we need to remember that Lucan himself has many of the faults attributed to *The Barons Warres*. Ben Jonson, twice in his conversations with William Drummond, says that "Lucan, taken in parts, was good . . . read altogether merited not the name of a poet."[8] Lucan's *Pharsalia* lacks the formal coherence we associate with epic. In addition, when Drayton revised his complaints as legends and *Mortimeriados* as *The Barons Warres*, he improved them as coherent, historical narratives, but literary verve was sacrificed.

Satire: *The Owle*

The Owle (1604) was entered in the Stationers' Register on 8 February 1604. We know that it was in print by 21 April 1604 because Juel Bent-Jensen has identified a transcript of the printed text dated 21 April 1604 (Tillotson, 283). The date of composition is more difficult to determine because Drayton included a note in the 1604 epistle "To the Reader," stating that *The Owle* was finished in 1603: "At which time (it gave place by my inforcement) undertaking then in the generall joye of the Kingdome, and my zeale to his Highnesse, to write his Majesties descent in a Poeme gratulatorie" (not reprinted in 1619, Tillotson, 181). Drayton's note would date the poem prior to James's accession on 24 March 1603, but this note may have been a politic effort on Drayton's part to suggest that the abuses described in *The Owle* were Elizabethan problems, which awaited James's wise solutions.

Even if some topical allusions remain elusive, Drayton's satire is pointed enough so that anyone with authority, power, or wealth could take offense. In certain instances his detailed portraits appear to refer to specific individuals. The Vulture sets legal traps for his victims, who are forced to pay fines or bribes in order to keep out of prison: "To buy his owne, accounts a Princely gift" (496). Some evidence supports the identification of the Vulture with Sir Robert Cecil. The pun on secretary, "secret" (444), identifies his position in the state. In the British Library copy of *The Owle* beside the stanzas having to do with the Vulture, there is a *C* written in a seventeenth-century hand that can be dated before 1640.[9]

The Bat assists the Vulture by entrapping his victims; he initiates a treasonous plot, but then reveals it to the authorities: "whereby himselfe he cleeres" (513). Beside the stanzas on the Bat, a *B* is written in the British Library copy. Tillotson and Newdigate have identified an allusion in Nathaniel Baxter's *Sir Philip Sydneys Ourania* (1606), suggesting that the Bat may be Sir Francis Bacon, who was popularly believed to have betrayed Essex:

> Learned *Drayton* hath told Madge-howlets tale,
> In covert verse of sweetest Madrigale.
> . . . .
> The Bat delights herselfe with Bacon best.
> (Newdigate, 132; Tillotson, 179)

The reference to the Bat's liking "Bacon best" indicates that at least Nathaniel Baxter believed the Bat to be a portrait of Sir Francis Bacon.

Having surveyed the ills in the court, country, and city, Drayton concludes *The Owle* with an allegory of the Essex rebellion (1,068–1,190). The royal Eagle, presumably James, interrupts this description of the "loathesome slime" of treason and advises a return to virtuous hierarchy in which the powerful care for the less privileged (1,190–1,242). *The Owle* concludes with a series of individualized portraits (1,243–1,304) that include the Falcon, who courageously keeps the kingdom safe; the immoral Throstle, who flatters lords; and the Cock, who combines "the Elegance and Act" (1,282). The Cock is a portrait of Sir Philip Sidney, whose eloquence and military prowess establish him as an ideal courtier. Drayton's uncompromising analysis of political and social corruption was published immediately before James's triumphal entry into London.

Moses in a Map of his Miracles

Drayton's divine poem, *Moses in a Map of his Miracles,* was entered in the Stationers' Register on 25 June 1604 and dedicated to Sir Walter Aston with the assurance that his "free Muse" required only Aston's support (Tillotson, 227). Drayton offers these "hallowed rimes" as "the vertuous payment of a worthier debt." He mentions that "ampler times" may allow him to offer "some glorious object," presumably *Poly-Olbion.* The sonnet concludes with the promise that this future "monument" will outlast steel and marble. Although dedicated to Aston, *Moses in a Map of his Miracles* demonstrates Drayton's initial eagerness to attract James's patronage. In addition to sponsoring an English translation of Du Bartas's *Judith,* James I had included both the French original and his translation of *Uranie* in *The Essays of a Prentice* (1584).[10]

Drawing on nonbiblical legends, Drayton romanticizes the accounts of Moses' birth and childhood in Egypt in the first book of *Moses in a Map of his Miracles.* The book concludes when Jehovah appears to Moses in a burning bush and charges him with leading the Hebrew people out of Egypt. Drayton begins book 2 with a description of the contest between Moses and Pharaoh's sorcerers. Moses wins, but Pharaoh refuses to permit the Hebrew people to leave. Drayton calls upon his Muse to lead him where "[n]o former foot did ever tract a way" (volume 3, line 63) and devotes the next 570 lines to minute and graphic descriptions of the Ten Plagues. He concludes his account of the horrors of the tenth plague with a moving allusion to the plague that devastated London in 1603:

> That sickly season, when I undertooke
> This composition faintly to supply,
> When thy affliction serv'd me for a booke,
> Whereby to modell Egypts miserie,
> When pallid horrour did possesse thy streete,
> Nor knew thy Children refuge where to have,
> Death them so soone in every place did meete,
> Unpeopling houses to possesse the grave.
>   (625–36)

In book 3 Drayton parallels the sea casting up the wreckage of Pharaoh's army with the "Castilian riches" (67) washed up on the shore after the defeat of the Spanish armada in 1588. The poem predictably concludes with Moses' death and arrival in the Promised Land. Drayton's experiment in writing heroic verse on a sacred subject was not a success. *Moses in a Map of his Miracles* contains some of his clumsiest writing, but he made almost no changes in the poem when he republished it in 1630 as *Moses his Birth and Miracles*.

Odes

Drayton's odes were entered in the Stationers' Register in a volume entitled *Poemes lyrick and pastoral* on 19 April 1606. The 1606 edition contained twelve odes, ten of which were reprinted in 1619 with many minor revisions; eight new odes were added in 1619. Drayton's generic description of the ode in his 1606 preface "To the Reader" anticipates the critical attention to genre, conventions, and decorum that fully informs the 1619 edition of his poems.

Claiming unique importance for Drayton's odes, Richard Hardin has argued that his odes best represent the kind of poet Drayton was. Hardin selects the ode "To the Virginian Voyage" and the "Ballad of the Battle of Agincourt" as Drayton's most characteristic and successful achievements.[11] Although persuasively argued in a fine critical study, this argument does not sufficiently acknowledge Drayton's literary aspirations. Even in his odes Drayton is less a patriot than an aspiring laureate, deploring an age that has become more suitable for satire than heroic verse. In "To Himselfe, and the Harpe," he begins by asserting his right as a poet to revive "th'old *Lyrick* kind." This assertion increases in political flavor as the poem progresses:

> Apollo, and the Nine,
> 　Forbid no Man their Shrine,
> . . . .
> For they be such curious Things,
> 　That they care not for Kings,
> And dare let them know it;
> Nor may he touch their Springs,
> 　That is not born a Poet.
> 　　　　　(11–12, 16–20)

Drayton's boast that poets "care not for Kings," and "dare let them know it" is revealing, especially when we consider that, six years earlier, he had praised James as a poet-king. By 1606 Drayton seems to feel that to be true to his muse, a poet must defy kings.

Even in his ode "To the Virginian Voyage" Drayton functions more as a poet lamenting his lack of heroic subject matter than as a patriot praising heroic exploration.[12] Those who embark on the Virginian voyage are "brave Heroique Minds" while those who remain in England are "loyt'ring Hinds" who "lurke" at home (5–6). The explorers are the "happy'st men" (51). Drayton interprets the Virginian voyage as an opportunity for his contemporaries to show themselves worthy of their own heroic past:

> And in Regions farre
> Such *Heroes* bring yee foorth,
>   As those from whom We came,
>   And plant Our name,
> Under that Starre
> Not knowne unto our North.
>   (55–60)

Just as the New World, those "Regions farre," will supply a setting for new heroes, there will also be "Laurel every where" (62). These heroes will require poets to sing of their triumphs in this new land where the laurel flourishes:

> APOLLO'S Sacred tree,
>   You it may see,
> A Poets Browes
> To crowne, that may sing there.
>   (63–66)

Even in this celebration of Virginia Drayton remains conscious of the "loyt'ring Hinds" who resist the challenge of exploration. The heroic achievements of the New World will nourish laurel trees, but in an ignoble England poetry can only turn to history for its subject matter.

Drayton does turn to history in the "Ballad of Agincourt," but the heroes who fought with Henry V are juxtaposed with Drayton's contemporaries:

> O, when shall *English* Men
> With such Acts fill a Pen,

> Or *England* breed againe,
> Such a King *Harry?*
> (117–20)

For Drayton the contrast between England's past and present is developed by its impact on the poet. Where are those heroic acts, Drayton asks, that would "fill a Pen"? Since Drayton uses the name Great Britain for England throughout *Poly-Olbion,* the play upon "England" and "English," as Richard Hardin suggests, may be intended as a gibe at the peace-loving Scottish James.

Patronage in Pastorals

Drayton's revision of *Idea The Shepheards Garland* (1593) was entered in the Stationers' Register on 19 April 1606 and first published with the odes in the quarto edition of *Poemes Lyrick and pastorall. Odes, Eglogs, The Man in the Moone* (1606). His 1606 revisions account for his uneasy relationship with the court throughout James's reign. As in *Idea The Shepheards Garland* patronage is a major theme in Drayton's 1606 pastorals, but he no longer hopes for a return of the golden age. He no longer believes that committed poets and worthy patrons will combine forces to support heroic values.

In the first eclogue Rowland comments on the injustice of the patronage system:

> Such are exalted basely that can faine,
> And none regards just *Rowland of the Rocke.*
> To those fat Pastures, others helthful keepe,
> Malice denyes me entrance with my sheepe.
> (Tillotson, 51–54)

Those who "faine," or pretend, are "exalted basely," but no one concerns himself with the fate of the "just" and plain-spoken Rowland.

While he does much to improve the praise of Idea in eclogue 5 and to make it clear that Idea is intended as the Idea of poetry, Drayton's most telling revisions involve the sixth eclogue of *Idea The Shepheards Garland,* revised as the eighth in 1606. This eclogue begins with a dialogue between Gorbo and Perkin concerning Fortune's inconstant favor. In the 1606 version Gorbo pointedly questions the injustice of the patronage system in which "wisemen" may be disgraced while a "barbarous asse" aspires to "high place and dignity" (27–28). When Gorbo asks who is responsible for

this clientage in which the unworthy are preferred, the questions artfully
imply that blind chance may not be to blame:

> What should I say, that Fortune is to blame,
> Or unto what should I impute the shame?
> (29–30)

This question is not answered until later in the eighth eclogue. Although
this eclogue, unlike the sixth eclogue of the 1593 pastorals, is not a panegyric on Mary Herbert, she is still praised. Faced with a period of unprece-
dented decadence, virtue has fled and taken refuge with the sister of Sir
Philip Sidney.

After praising Mary Herbert, Drayton comments generally on the fickle
behavior of women and moves first to an invective against Lucy, Countess of
Bedford, and second to an attack on James, the reigning monarch. Rowland
(Drayton), a loyal and high-minded poet, has been betrayed by his faithless
patroness Selena (Lucy). The name Selena, an alternate name for the goddess
of the moon, plays on the etymological meaning of Lucy as light. (In 1595
Drayton had indulged in similar wordplay with Lucy's name to compliment
her in *Endimion and Phoebe*.) Selena has deserted Rowland for "deceitfull
Cerberon," the three-headed dog associated with hell (Tillotson, 189).

Rowland is enraged because Selena, who "purpos'd to have raysed" his estate, has chosen to favor Cerberon:

> And to deceitefull *Cerberon* she cleaves
> That beastly clowne to vile of to be spoken,
> And that good shepheard wilfully she leaves
> And falsly al her promises hath broken,
> And al those beautyes whilom that her graced,
> With vulgar breath perpetually defaced.
> (Tillotson, 189)

He contrasts the flower-crowned Eliza, Queen Elizabeth, with Selena, who
causes flowers to wither when they touch her brow.

> What daintie flower yet ever was there found
> Whose smell or beauty mighte the sence delighɩ
> Wherwith *Eliza* when she lived was crowned
> In goodly chapplets he for her not dighte.
> (Tillotson, 189)

The dainty flowers that crowned Eliza, the "goodly chapplets," conflict with Selena's nature,

> Which became withered soon as ere shee ware them
> So ill agreeing with the brow that bare them.
>
> (Tillotson, 189)

By emphasizing the "withering" effect of Lucy's brow, Drayton is accusing her of having a malign influence on "goodly" poetry. In a tone adopted by no other English Renaissance poet toward a powerful patroness, he curses Lucy, calling on "age" to make her old and ugly:

> Let age sit soone and ugly on her brow,
> No sheepheards praises living let her have
> To her last end noe creature pay one vow
> Nor flower be strew'd on her forgotten grave,
> And to the last of all devouring tyme
> Nere be her name remembred more in rime.
>
> (Tillotson, 189)

Drayton completes his invective by dooming Lucy to oblivion, "Nere be her name remembered more in rime." He was serious about taking back his former promises that his verse would preserve Lucy's fame. He never alludes to Lucy again, and in 1619 he deliberately misrepresents her patronage of his early work. The passage containing the invective against the Countess of Bedford was omitted from the 1619 folio but not necessarily because he forgave her. By 1619 Lucy had lost her beauty during a severe case of small pox, which settled in her eye socket and for a time jeopardized her sight.

By 1606 Drayton's optimism about James's accession had given way to bitter disappointment. Using the name Olcon for James, he contrasts his earlier idealistic expectations with his disillusionment. Olcon seemed a "Phoebus" to the shepherds, and Rowland "esteemed" him as a "god":

> For, after *ROWLAND,* as it had beene *PAN,*
> Onely to *OLCON* every Shepheard ran.
>
> (95–96)

In a probable allusion to his 1600 sonnet praising James, Drayton suggests that the "rurall Rout" (94) followed his "forward pen" when they later welcomed James.

The second stanza criticizes James for neglecting his duties. He has abandoned his flocks to the wolf and fox and pays no attention to his "Bag-pipes":

> But he forsakes the Heard-groome and his Flocks,
> Nor of his Bag-pipes takes at all no keepe,
> But to the sterne Wolfe and deceitfull Fox,
> Leaves the poore Shepheard and his harmelesse Sheepe.
>
> (97–100)

As with Lucy, Drayton denies James the praise he had previously addressed to the new king:

> And all those Rimes that he of *OLCON* sung,
> The Swayne disgrac'd, participate his wrong.
>
> (101–2)

Drayton never forgave James for his neglect. In *Poly-Olbion,* dedicated first to Prince Henry in 1613 and then to Prince Charles in 1622, he omits James from his list of great British rulers.

Drayton devotes the remainder of the eighth eclogue to eulogizing patronesses, who, though of lower rank than Lucy, remain loyal: "And praysing some may happily inflame" others (107). He first praises the virtue of Lucy's kinswomen, the Goodere sisters, Lady Frances Goodere and Lady Anne Rainsford. He identifies Anne Goodere, Lady Rainsford, as Idea, but the identification does not suggest that Drayton nursed an unrequited love for her:

> The yonger then, her Sister not lesse good,
> Bred where the other lastly doth abide,
> Modest *IDEA,* flowre of Womanhood,
> That *Rowland* hath so highly deified
>
> (115–18)

The context of this passage is important to its interpretation. Drayton's identification of Anne Goodere Rainsford as Idea in 1606 serves the purpose of eliminating Lucy from his verse. By identifying her less prominent relative as Idea, he has completed the process of consigning Lucy to oblivion.

It is also worth noting that the heir to Polesworth, Frances Goodere's husband, the younger Sir Henry, is not included in this compliment. Since John and Francis Beaumont are praised along with their sister Elizabeth (138–

44), the omission may be related to Sir Henry Goodere's service in the household of Lucy, Countess of Bedford.[13] Drayton may have attributed his loss of Lucy's patronage to Goodere.

In 1593 Drayton had concluded his pastorals with a portrait of Rowland as a lovesick swain, but in 1606 he is depicted as the victim of thwarted aspiration and untapped talents. He cries out against Fortune and Time who "at first encourag'd" his desire, but "lastly against me lewdly doe conspire" (55–60). Nature, he blames, for "prodigally" wasting her gifts on "me infortunatest Swayne" (61–62), and then asks:

> Vertue in me why was thou plac'd in vaine?
> If to the World predestined a prey.
>
> (63–64)

Not even stoicism, the tonic most often prescribed for suffering, consoles Drayton for the frustration of his laureate ambitions. His likely death is mourned only by the groves, rivers, birds, and beasts. He is left alone with his dog Whitefoote to whom he says farewell:

> The Time is come, Thou must thy Master leave,
> Whom the vile World shall never more deceave.
>
> (95–96)

Heart broken, Rowland dies.

The pastorals appear in the volume entitled *Poemes Lyrick and pastorall* (1606) and dedicated to Sir Walter Aston, but the dedication is strangely worded: "To the deserving memory of my most esteemed Patron and friend, Sir Walter Aston" (Tillotson, 148). Since Aston was alive in 1606, the allusion to his "deserving memory" may indicate that after Drayton's publication of *The Owle* (1604), Aston's patronage was less substantial. Drayton's invective did not attract commendatory poems from his contemporaries, but contemporary references to his honest and straightforward behavior are likely in part to have been inspired by his stand on patronage.[14]

On 12 October 1607 Drayton entered *The Legend of Great Cromwell* in the Stationers' Register, and his *Cromwell* was later included in *Mirror for Magistrates* (1610). In *Cromwell* Drayton returns to the ottava rima stanza of *The Barons Warres* and to the complaint, but as his title, *The Legend of Great Cromwell*, suggests, he now thinks of this genre as a legend. *Cromwell* examines the Protestant Reformation with a somber objectivity uncharacteristic of Drayton's earlier historical writing. He condemns the spoiling of

the monasteries and depicts Henry VIII as bigamous and morally exped-
ient. Shakespeare's *Henry VIII* (1613) offers a far more politic view of
James's ancestor. Drayton portrays the Reformation as fueled by greed and
prejudice, but, again, there were no reprisals from the authorities. His
antiroyalist stance in *Cromwell,* however, added to the growing evidence
that patronage of Michael Drayton would be incompatible with preferment
in the Jacobean court.

Chapter Five
"Herculean toyle":
Poly-Olbion

Drayton's *Poly-Olbion,* the major work that he hoped would insure his endur-
ing reputation, surveys in alexandrine couplets the geography and history of
Great Britain. An entire volume (604 pages) of the standard edition of
Drayton is devoted to *Poly-Olbion,* which was published in two parts, the first
appearing in 1612, the second in 1622. The elaborate apparatus accompanying *Poly-Olbion* suggests how much of Drayton's literary ambition was in-
vested in this poem.[1] He includes a verse argument and a map of the region
covered for each song, marginal glosses, annotations by the learned antiquary
John Selden, and a Table directing the reader to "those occurrences of *Story*
and *Antiquitie,* whereunto the Course of the Volume easily leades not" (i*).[2]
This index supplements the maps by organizing material in terms of historical time rather than topographical space.

The subtitle to *Poly-Olbion* promises "Chorographicall Description of
Tracts, Rivers, Mountaines, Forests, and other Parts of this renowned Isle of
Great Britaine, With intermixture of the most Remarquable Stories, Antiq-
uities, Wonders, Rarityes, Pleasures, and Commodities of the Same" (i*).
The term *chorography,* although widely used in the seventeenth century, is
now unfamiliar. Chorographical works mapped the topography and history
of a county or district.

The title *Poly-Olbion* puns on "Poly" (*very* or *much*) and "Olbion" as
Albion (*England*) and Greek (*happy* or *fortunate*).[3] The poem before the
frontispiece plays on this complicated etymology: Albion is placed "[i]n
Happy site, in *Neptunes* armes embras't" (ii*). The female figure who repre-
sents Albion is labeled "Great Britaine," signifying the union of England,
Scotland, and Wales. Since the union of England and Scotland as Great Brit-
ain was a project dear to the heart of James VI of Scotland who became James
I of England, Drayton's identification of the figure Albion as Great Britain
could be interpreted as an accommodation to royal power. Little else in *Poly-
Olbion* supports such an interpretation.

The frontispiece to *Poly-Olbion* (1612), engraved by William Hole, is reproduced with the permission of the Henry E. Huntington Library, San Marino, California

Frontispiece

The frontispiece to *Poly-Olbion,* an engraving by William Hole, serves a number of political and aesthetic functions.[4] Drayton personifies Britain as a female body, but his treatment of the world-body metaphor does not acknowledge the tradition that the monarch had two bodies, one of which represented the kingdom.[5] Britain is depicted as a royal woman whose pose strongly resembles that of Elizabeth in the frontispiece to Christopher Saxon's *Survey of England and Wales* (1579).[6] The symbolism of the frontispiece also recalls the many iconographical celebrations of Elizabeth, especially the Ditchley portrait, in which she stands on the map of her island kingdom. Britain's clothing is covered by hills and valleys, symbolically representing her topography. In her left arm she holds a cornucopia for plenty and in her right a scepter for power. Britain is seated on a rocky throne; a fleet of ships covers the surrounding ocean, recalling Britain's mastery of the seas under Elizabeth. In song 18, the concluding song of *Poly-Olbion* (1612), Drayton supplies a catalog of valiant military leaders. By 1604 James had made peace with Spain, and by 1606 he had begun to favor and actively explore a Catholic marriage for his son, Prince Henry. His pro-Spanish foreign policy and his failure to support the Virginia Company had already antagonized many, although the opposition increased in the 1620s with the loss of the Palatinate.

Britain is framed by a triumphal arch with statues of armored figures representing the four conquerors of Britain: legendary Brute, the nephew of Aeneas; Julius Caesar; Hengist, leader of the victorious Saxons; William of Normandy. These conquests supply the historical logic of the first part of *Poly-Olbion.* James traced his descent from the Norman conquerors, but his coat of arms does not appear on this frontispiece. His foreign policy, which aimed at keeping Britain out of European conflict, rendered his portrayal as a warrior king unlikely.[7] By 1612 the militant Protestant party, represented under Elizabeth by the Earl of Leicester, Sir Philip Sidney, and the Earl of Essex, had adopted Prince Henry as its leader.

Drayton dedicates *Poly-Olbion* (1612) to Prince Henry, who is described as Britain's "best hope, and the world's delight" (iv). In the portrait of Henry facing the dedication, he is pictured with a pike, sword, and helmet, suggesting his heroic values. Prince Henry represented the "best hope" of those who wanted Britain to involve itself in European politics and who opposed alliance with Spain.[8] An admirer of Sir Walter Ralegh, Henry also endorsed colonization of the New World. Since voyages of discovery and exploration excited Drayton's imagination, he could see in Henry the ruler of a future British empire.

The Politics of Humanist and Antiquarian Sources

The first part of *Poly-Olbion* (songs 1–18) was published between 9 May 1612, when John Selden signed the Preface to his learned annotations, and 6 November 1612, when Prince Henry died. Although the second part of *Poly-Olbion* was not published until a decade later in 1622, Drayton had completed "[s]undry other Songs . . . though yet not so perfect that I dare commit them to publique censure" in 1612 (vi*). Newdigate thinks that the work was complete by November 1618 (Tillotson, 161); Hebel suggests 1619 (4:ix), but Drayton did not find a printer for songs 19–30 until 1622.

Humanist and antiquarian interests are difficult to separate because, like William Camden, many of the leading British antiquarians were humanists interested in Roman ruins and classical history, as well as in recording and preserving native culture. *Poly-Olbion* illustrates the patriotic enthusiasm that challenged Renaissance writers to reproduce everything in English that had ever been attempted by classical authors. Of the classical and continental poems that may have served as models for Drayton, the most important are the *Periegesis* of Dionysius, written in Greek hexameters but translated into English prose in 1572, and the *Mosella,* recording a downstream journey by the fourth-century Gallo-Roman Decimus Magnus Ausonius.

Drayton's friend Francis Meres illustrates the cultural nationalism of sixteenth-century England. His list of classical authors and English counterparts alludes to *Poly-Olbion,* indicating that Drayton had begun his poem fourteen years before the first part appeared (75). In *Poly-Olbion* Drayton tries to do for the landscape and culture of Great Britain what Meres had tried to do for English letters: he sets out to show that there is an English equivalent for everything classical. In song 10 he defends the authority of the chronicle of Geoffrey of Monmouth and insists upon the authenticity of legends about the Trojan origins of Britain. He claims that the story of Brute was carefully researched and examined by judges, unlike the "fabulous" tales "devised by the *Greeks*" (10.256). More than decorative classical allusion is at stake; Drayton wants to legitimize the cultural history of Britain.

Throughout *Poly-Olbion* the heroes, events, and geographical wonders of the classical world are used as touchstones to demonstrate the importance of Great Britain. The legends of King Arthur supply material for a British epic, an epic that could have surpassed the Homeric epics if the British bards had made use of their native heroic tales (song 3). The religion of the Druids is stronger than that of the Romans (song 6). Lemster wool is more valuable than the golden fleece (song 7). Malvern Hill is far more glorious than Mount Olympus, and there are more curves in the Wye river than in the fabled classical Meander (song 7). Guy of Warwick is the English Hercules; the Danes invaded England with all the ferocity with which the Greeks invaded Troy (song 12). The naval heroes of Britain can only be compared with the Greek Argonauts (song 19). English history and geography are viewed through classical lenses.

In spite of arguments that the two parts of *Poly-Olbion* differ in focus and tone, the same kinds of comparisons continue in the second part of Drayton's *Poly-Olbion* (1622). Neptune may leave his fair Thetis to embrace the Ouze river (song 20). Holland Marsh smells worse than the Acherusian Fen, the underworld source of the classical river Acheron (song 25). The Maid Marian of Sherwood Forest is England's own Diana (song 26). Drayton even concludes his poem by comparing his efforts as an author in writing *Poly-Olbion* with the labors of Hercules (song 30). These classical allusions invite the reader to approach *Poly-Olbion* as a chorographical *Aeneid*.

Drayton's preface describes his poem as a series of tableaux, of "artificiall caves, cut out of the most naturall Rock," which will show the "ancient people of this Ile" in their "lively images" (v*). For Drayton, the classical stories and allusions act as influential forms and references, as "artificial caves" that help him shape his poem out of native materials. These native materials derive primarily from the British antiquarian movement. Drayton was well acquainted with John Stow, William Camden, and John Selden, key figures in this movement, but he also drew upon the research of an earlier generation of scholars.[9]

Prior to the seventeenth century antiquarian scholarship had traditionally been under the monarch's patronage. John Leland, who actually called himself *"Antiquarius,"* was given a royal commission in 1533 to examine libraries and other repositories in order to draw together those sources and materials from which an accurate history of England could be compiled. He intended to make a map of England and Wales and then to write a book entitled *De Antiquitate Britannica* or *Civilis Historia,* organized geographically by shires and relating important local history.

Two of Leland's poems illustrate the close patronage links between chorography and the monarch. His poetic *Genethliacon* (1543) combines topography with royal compliment. After celebrating the birth of Edward VI, who was to receive the honorary titles of Prince of Wales, Duke of Cornwall, and Earl of Chester, Leland presents a topographical survey concentrating on the geographical areas associated with Edward's titles. Leland's *Cygnea*

Cantio (1546), another influence on Drayton, combines topography and Tudor history, concluding with an oration praising Henry VIII.[10]

As late as 1598 the monarch was still expected to sponsor antiquarian studies. John Norden appealed to Elizabeth in the expectation of royal patronage when his *Speculum Britanniae* (1598) was in danger of languishing for lack of funds. His appeal was unsuccessful, but his expectations show that the tradition of royal support for chorography was just beginning to erode. By the seventeenth century, the Society of Antiquaries, founded in 1586, was not patronized by the monarch. The Society was denied official recognition by Elizabeth in 1601, and James not only refused official recognition, but also insisted that the private meetings of the Society be abandoned.[11] The Society was disbanded in 1607, and James did not favor its reestablishment in 1614.

Camden, a central figure in antiquarian research and the most direct influence on Drayton's *Poly-Olbion,* prided himself on having remained independent of royal patronage and of withstanding "present preferments."[12] By the time that *Poly-Olbion* (1612) appeared, chorography, formerly patronized by the monarch, was regarded as subversive, even more suspect than chronicle history. Although Drayton's omission of James from the catalog of English monarchs in song 17 has long been recognized, this omission has been attributed to Drayton's personal pique over lack of preferment. That Drayton uses antiquarian sources to comment on seventeenth-century politics has gone unnoticed. The female frontispiece and dedication to Prince Henry discussed above, however, signal his intentions.

Camden's *Britannia,* Drayton's principal source, was issued in an octavo edition in 1586, but revised and added to until the folio edition of 1607. Drayton uses Camden's county-by-county organization in *Poly-Olbion,* but he moves from southwest England to Wales rather than to southeast England. This geographical variation enables him to dwell on the Arthurian legends, which he cherished, and to introduce his own views on the historical sequence of conquests: Trojan-Briton, Roman, Saxon, and Norman.[13]

Most studies of Drayton's handling of Welsh history have concerned the identification of sources.[14] Drayton's insistence in songs 6 and 10 that the Welsh were the original inhabitants of Britain and descendants of the Trojans has been traced to his study of Welsh antiquarian scholars. Yet, Drayton's annotator, the antiquary John Selden, in his preface explicitly says that he has supported the theory of the *"Trojan Brute* . . . (but as an Advocat for the Muse) . . . disclaiming in it if alleg'd for my own Opinion" (viii*). Why, then, does Drayton so firmly insist upon the importance of the Trojan descent of Brutus and the primacy of Welsh culture? First, unlike many of his humanist predecessors and contemporaries, he respected medieval culture and so gave great credence to medieval chronicles. In song 6 he attacks those who disparage antiquity because some "slight fictions" are mixed "with the truth" (6.278). These men, he claims, are like the iconoclasts, who because they see a cross or saint in the window, will tear down the church (6.301–4).

Second, Drayton identifies the culture of the early Britons as the authentic past, but acknowledges that the early conquests of Britain by the Saxons and the Romans contributed to the land and culture. In contrast, the Normans are the villains who come from France to oppress England. In songs 11 through 13 Drayton shows that the Anglo-Saxon conquest infused a warlike strength in the inhabitants and brought Christianity to the island. In the 1560s and 1570s a group of antiquarian scholars including Laurence Nowell, William Lambarde, Archbishop Matthew Parker, and his secretary John Jocelyn had inaugurated Anglo-Saxon studies.[15] Because of this research, Drayton recognized that the Anglo-Saxons and the Normans belonged to one Germanic people, but he treats the two conquests very differently.[16] He condemns the Norman Conquest because he believes that the Normans deprived the native British of fundamental liberties.

In *Poly-Olbion* Drayton's anti-James, anti-Scottish bias is "displaced" and becomes anti-Norman. The Norman Conquest established the ruling house from which James traced his ancestry, as is noted in the poem on the frontispiece (ii*). Drayton's anti-Norman bias is shared by Selden, and in this instance the poem and the annotations complement each other by showing that the Norman Conquest caused the abrogation of the traditional liberties of the Britons. The ancient freedoms of the original British are maintained against the conquering Normans who try to eradicate the charters protecting the liberties of free men. King John is opposed by the barons because he tried to drive into "slavery" the "freest borne *English* blood" (17.175–76).

In certain instances Drayton deliberately includes passages likely to offend his Scottish king. He unabashedly celebrates the English kings and heroes who conquered the Scottish (17.186–92; 18.130–34). By 1612 Robert Carr had already begun his spectacular rise in rank. James's preference for male favorites was generally acknowledged. In his earlier historical treatments of the reign of Edward II Drayton had treated Edward's death with discretion. In *Poly-Olbion* the description is brutally indecorous:

> For that preposterous sinne wherein he did offend,
> In his posteriour parts had his preposterous end.
> (17.199–200)

As in Drayton's *Cromwell* (1607), James's ancestor, Henry VIII is a self-indulgent wastrel, "who lov'd *Polygamy*" (17.320). He concludes his catalog of English monarchs with Elizabeth, and every line of the tribute to Elizabeth contrives to disparage James's foreign policy. Drayton could have celebrated Elizabeth for reestablishing the Protestant religion, but instead he praises her for building an empire. Elizabeth was a great monarch because she aided the Flemish and French against Spain, conquered Ireland, supported Portugal against Spain, humbled Spain by taking Cadiz, and explored the New World. Elizabeth is celebrated as a fit successor to Edward I and Henry V, who remain Drayton's favorites among the English kings.

Land and People

Although *Poly-Olbion* has been described as a patriotic work, celebrating the values of the "country" as opposed to those of the "court," the applicability of these terms to seventeenth-century literature and politics has been questioned by Kevin Sharpe.[17] In the case of *Poly-Olbion* these terms are misleading. Drayton's celebration of Great Britain is not a partisan work; he wants to forge a record of national consciousness, but he is highly critical of James's administration. This tension is maintained in a structure that renders *Poly-Olbion* a strangely disjunctive work. The land of Great Britain illustrates discord resolving into concord, but the tranquillity of the land stands in sharp contrast to the turmoil of the people.

In his preface Drayton uses pastoral imagery to suggest that in *Poly-Olbion* he will idealize the landscape of Britain. The reader is invited to go up on a hill and from that prospect see the "old and later times" (v*). The landscape that Drayton describes has an Arcadian simplicity and beauty: we see "delicate embrodered Meadowes, often veined with gentle sliding Brooks" (v*). Lovely nude nymphs bathe in crystalline streams. The human figures are the "harmlesse Shepheards" of literature who sing to their "gazing flocks" (v*). Commenting upon Drayton's idealized landscape, Stella Revard has suggested that he uses pastoral personification throughout *Poly-Olbion* to establish a literary ideal.[18] His hills and rivers become characters in a pastoral masque. Likewise, Barbara Ewell observes that Drayton uses "England as body metaphor" to idealize and eternalize his subject.[19] Both authors observe that the rivalries among personifications of the landscape, rivers, hills, and forests, are resolved harmoniously through Drayton's use of *discordia concors*.

While there is ample textual evidence that Drayton wanted to create an idealized landscape, his historical catalogs and orations on politics and poetry contradict this ideal. The body of the land, the landscape of Britain, is idealized in *Poly-Olbion,* but human nature and history are not. The four conquests of the ancient Britons by Brute, Caesar, Hengist, and William of Normandy dominate history in the first part of *Poly-Olbion.* Near the conclusion of song 18 Drayton dramatically focuses on British liberty. Kent, a bastion of freedom, revolts against the "servile yoke" of the Normans and restores Kentish liberties (30.731–33):

> Not suffering forraine Lawes should thy free Customes bind,
> Then onely showd'st thy selfe of th'ancient *Saxon* kind.
> Of all the *English* Shires be thou surnam'd the Free.
>
> (30.735–57)

In contrast to men, the land understands the reciprocity of political hierarchy. In song 7 Malvern Hill rules the subject hills with graciousness while they respond with reverence. In song 9 the nymphs of the lakes challenge the authority of the mountains, creating a "faction" (9.166). The great Snowdon appeals to natural law and to an ideal hierarchy in which monarch and subjects fulfill their responsibilities.

An Anatomy of Time

Critical studies of *Poly-Olbion* have focused upon two issues: its overall structure as a poem and the relationship between the two parts of *Poly-Olbion* (1612, 1622).[20] These studies clarify important facets of Drayton's poetic design, but the diversity of *Poly-Olbion* remains a problem. Drayton has tried to combine Ovidian whimsy, chronicle history, and political orations with analysis of the cultural function of art and literature. These disparate elements do not add up to a unified poem. At least one critic has suggested that Drayton's muse fulfills the function of the protagonist or hero in an epic poem by becoming a focal point for the reader's attention, but the muse's function is too diffuse to unify the poem.[21] Drayton's muse, a concrete figure who exists apart from the poet, travels around the country acting as an agent for prosopopoeia. She enables rivers, valleys, and hills to speak, and the landscape also addresses the muse, as does the poet, when he urges her not to falter near the end of the second part.

Drayton's objectification of the muse is related to his decision to advance the narrative by dialogue and oration. *Poly-Olbion* concentrates rhetorically on speeches and conversations, in contrast to, for example, Wordsworth's *Prelude,* a poetic meditation that the reader overhears. The rhetorical design of *Poly-Olbion* requires that we approach this poem as an address to the reader, not as a self-contained organic whole. We need to approach Drayton's *Poly-Olbion* as we do Burton's *Anatomy of Melancholy*. Drayton has even supplied a subject index to facilitate thematic reading. We are not supposed to concentrate on the text of the poem and ignore the prefaces and elaborate chorographical illustrations.

Approached as a loosely organized set of variations on the central theme of time, *Poly-Olbion* can engage the reader's interest. It offers an anatomy of time, exposing the tension between past achievement and present memory. Pictures of the landscape never come to life, but we hear an insistent voice reminding us that poetry contributes to and preserves culture. Another voice reminds us that culture can be lost, never to be recovered. More vulnerable than the land, the monuments of human achievement may lose their meaning if they are not preserved. Drayton argues that culture must be interpreted and preserved, and *Poly-Olbion* itself becomes his exemplum.

Art That Remembers

A poet as concerned as Drayton was with preserving the past inevitably recognized that time could erase the memory of men's triumphs and defeats. His profound concern with mutability prompts him to treat monuments from the past as symbols. His approach to Stonehenge, for example, diverges significantly from those of John Selden and Samuel Daniel. Faced with an enigmatic mass of stones, they set out to distinguish truth from legend. In his annotation on Stonehenge in song 3, John Selden quotes from Sir Philip Sidney:

> But so confus'd that neyther any eye
> Can count them just, nor reason[?] try,
> What force brought them to so unlikely ground.
> (4:60)

Selden eagerly tries to solve the two mysteries that he identifies: how and why the great stones came to stand on Salisbury Plain. He tells us that the Saxons used treachery to destroy the Britons in a battle on the plain; later, the stones were transported from a hill near Kildare in Ireland as a "trophy, not of victory, but of wronged innocencie" (4:60). Selden next considers the monument's construction. Acknowledging that Stonehenge may have occurred naturally, he thinks it more likely that the stones are held together artificially.

In contrast, Drayton regards the heap of huge stones, some lying in the earth, others standing erect, and yet others lying across them, as the ruin of a monument, as a remnant of some former, much grander marker:

> Dull heape, that thus thy head above the rest doost reare,
> Precisely yet not know'st who first did place thee there.
>   (3.53–58)

Samuel Daniel's meditation on Stonehenge in *Musophilus* (1599) combines Selden's antiquarian and Drayton's poetic approach to Stonehenge. He first sifts through the legends that Selden reports, scoffing at the fabulous story that the stones were brought by demonic power from Africa to Ireland in one night and then transported to Britain by Merlin's magic. Alluding to the Saxon leader Hengist and his treachery against the Britons, Daniel interprets Stonehenge as a monument to deceitful antiquity and to the ignorance of later times: "With this old Legend then credulitie / Holdes her content, and closes vp her care" (365–66).[22]

Like Drayton, Daniel emphasizes the silence of the stones, but he is interested in the fabulous legends that they have inspired. For him Stonehenge symbolizes the futility of seeking to learn the truth about antiquity. Drayton, on the other hand, regards the fabled Stonehenge as a testimonial to the way in which time can erase the records of culture.

> Ill did those mightie men to trust thee with their storie,
> That hast forgot their names, who rear'd thee for their glorie
> For all their wondrous cost, thou that hast serv'd them so,
> What tis to trust to Tombes, by thee we easely know.
>   (3.61–64)

For Drayton, one of the principal functions of art is to preserve the memory of human achievement. Men cannot trust "Tombes" to insure their immortality. Stonehenge is a "dull heape," a silent pile of stones, the emblem of what becomes of forgotten culture.

Poetry: The Cause and Memory of Culture

Drayton was distressed by the lack of contemporary interest in the first part of *Poly-Olbion,* and in the second part he probes deeply into the poet's relation to his audience, exploring the social function of poetry. In song 21 he offers a remarkably clear assessment of public poetry. Poetry, he claims, should be mimetic; it should imitate life. Employing the traditional analogy between poetry and painting, Drayton suggests that the most that "Art doth strive to doe" is to express the life of its subject:

> What is of Paynters said, is of true Poets rife,
> That he which doth expresse things neerest to the life,
> Doth touch the very poynt, nor needs he adde thereto:
> For that the utmost is, that Art doth strive to doe.
>   (191–94)

The poet, like the painter, should "touch the very poynt." Drayton's insistence upon the mimetic function of poetry derives from his concept of the role of the poet as civilizer.

To illustrate the social role of the poet, Drayton turns to the myth of Orpheus whose playing persuaded the rocks and trees to follow him. The moral of this fable, Drayton says, is that Orpheus' music civilized those who had previously lacked culture:

> . . . his knowledge drew
> The stony, blockish rout, that nought but rudenesse knew,
> T'imbrace a civill life, by his inticing Layes.
>   (197–99)

Elaborating upon his interpretation of this myth, Drayton observes that if Orpheus, the bringer of civilization, had deliberately tried to keep from communicating with his audience, behaving "like many of these dayes, / Which to be understood, doe take in it disdaine" (21.200–201), then he would have been dismissed by other men as a madman. Orpheus then would have "been a veryer blocke, then those to whom he sung" (21.206). Mimetic art communicates with its audience, allowing poetry to exercise its civilizing function. By imitating the actions of men, mimetic poetry also preserves the memory of civilization.

The spokesman for Drayton's views is the river Cam that flows by Cambridge University. Learning, Drayton suggests, is essential for a poet. The Cam, a friend of the Muses, has heard that the Muses are concerned about how the poets who are Apollo's priests have been treated by the world. In Cam's tirade against the "worthlesse world" (126) we see juxtaposed Drayton's noble view of the poet and his contempt for the Jacobean literary scene: "He is a god, compar'd with ordinary men" (140); he lives in a realm removed from "worldly cares" (142):

When not the greatest King, should he his treasure raine,
The Muses sacred gifts, can possibly obtaine;
No, were he Monarch of the universall earth,
Except that gift from heaven, be breath'd into his birth.

(147–50)

Elevating the poet over the monarch, he also insists upon the divine inspiration of poets. Poets outrank kings, including perhaps King James, who regarded himself as divinely appointed. The poet has powers that even kings may envy, for poetic gifts cannot be bought. By 1622, the king's favorite George Villiers, Duke of Buckingham, was flagrantly exploiting the patronage system; earlier sales of titles and offices appeared restrained in retrospect.

After dismissing the materialists who undervalue poetry and attacking those who write without vocation, ideas, or craft, Drayton rejects poets who do not fulfill the high ideals of their vocation. Those who are "rightly christned" in the "*Helliconian* Fount" do not become flattering court poets: ". . . such as basely sooth the Humour of the Time, / And slubberingly patch up some slight and shallow Rime" (167–68). Poets who write nothing but verse epistles to prominent courtiers and entertainments for the court betray the high ideals of poetry.

Speaking as a craftsman who had reworked the sonnets that make up *Idea* (1619) for a quarter of a century, Drayton objects as well to the metrics and versification of those he labels "Mimick Apes" (171). Their verses, he says, "hobling runne, as with disjoynted bones, / And make a viler noyse, then carts upon the stones" (173–74). These comments suggest how much Drayton valued smoothness in verse. Poetry should be written in lines that "gliding flow in state" (186). He prefers sounds that are "fine and smooth" and sense that is "full and strong" (188). Drayton may have selected the alexandrine couplet for *Poly-Olbion* in order to achieve this effect. He would have felt that the weight of his subject matter required a flowing and stately meter.[23]

Drayton as Literary Critic

Michael Drayton deserves credit for introducing the important critical distinction that we make between "public" and "cabinet" or coterie poetry. In 1612 he developed this critical distinction, now used routinely to differentiate the poetry of Spenser from the poetry of Donne. In the preface addressed "To the Generall Reader" at the beginning of the first part of *Poly-Olbion* (1612) Drayton acknowledges that the kind of poem he has written differs from "cabinet" poetry: "In publishing this Essay of my poeme, there is this great disadvantage against me; that it commeth out at this time when Verses are wholly deduc't to Chambers, and nothing esteem'd in this lunatique Age, but what is kept in Cabinets, and must only passe by Transcription" (vi*). Drayton recognized that the learning concentrated in *Poly-Olbion* would make the poem unpopular with those unwilling to "seeke after more, then dull and slothfull ignorance may easily reach unto" (vi*). By 1622 when the second part of *Poly-Olbion* appeared, Drayton had become even more concerned about the vogue of cabinet poetry.

In song 21 Drayton offers an invective against cabinet poets. These poets are not the "Muses only heires" but "Bastards" (5, 6):

> Inforcing things in Verse for Poesie unfit,
> Mere filthy stuffe, that breakes out of the sores of wit:
> What Poet reckes the praise upon such Anticks heap'd,
> Or envies that their lines, in Cabinets are kept?
> Though some fantasticke foole promove their ragged Rymes,
> And doe transcribe them o'er a hundred severall times, . . .
>   (175–82)

Drayton's phrase, "filthy stuffe, that breakes out of the sores of wit," attacks the school of Donne. He admits that coterie poetry is popular; it can be kept in cabinets and transcribed "o'er a hundred severall times" (182), but he remains convinced that it is "lewd beggery trash, nay very gibbrish" (184).

For Drayton, the ideal poet had to sing sweetly, but he also had to address those values that underlie and preserve civilization. He rejected the private and difficult poetry, transcribed and stored in cabinets, because, for Drayton, good poetry enticed men to "imbrace a civill life." He beautifully suggests this when the River Charwell, who is a "curious Maker" (15.222) or fine poet, delivers a eulogy to the hills, rivers, and valleys:

> And as the earth doth us in her owne bowels nourish;
> So every thing, that growes by us, doth thrive and flourish.
> To godly vertuous men, we wisely likened are:
> To be so in themselves, that do not only care;
> But by a sacred power, which goodnesse doth awaite,
> Doe make those vertuous too, that them associate.
>   (15.275–80)

Just as the rivers nourish the land, the poet must inspire and report the acts of "godly vertuous men." Poetry nourishes the human community, publishing the goodness that connects the past and future.

Eden Brook

In song 30, at the conclusion of the second part, Drayton introduces again the ideas that dominated his description of Stonehenge. He describes a fascinating set of stones, resembling a monument from an earlier age, near the bank of a lovely brook called Eden:

> Stones seventie seven stand, in manner of a Ring,
> Each full ten foot in height, but yet the strangest thing,
> Their equall distance is, the circle that compose,
> Within which other stones lye flat, which doe inclose
> The bones of men long dead, (as there the people say).
> (319–23)

Drayton moralizes over a second monument of stones nine feet high, a mile in length, mourning their anonymity.

> The victories for which these Trophies were begun,
> From darke oblivion thou, O Time shouldst have protected;
> For mighty were their minds, them thus that first erected.
> (327–30)

When Drayton summoned up the image of Stonehenge in the first part of *Poly-Olbion,* those silent stones recalled heroic achievements; they hinted at a past that had not been fully recorded. By 1622 when he completed his thirtieth song, the last to be published, Drayton's vision had grown darker: the stones near Eden Brook tell no story; no one will ever be able to decipher their history. Mutability has triumphed. For Drayton, the monument near Eden Brook illustrates how time plunges human aspiration and victory into "darke oblivion."

Drayton's description of the ring of stones near Eden Brook, a haunting monument whose history has not survived, renders the unfinished conclusion of *Poly-Olbion* especially moving. His truly Herculean attempt to preserve the trophies and history of Great Britain from the ravages of time did not especially interest his contemporaries when the second part appeared. His 1622 preface addressed "To Any That Will Read It" underlines his awareness that Time had not only defaced the monuments of British history, but had also undermined the audience for his kind of public poetry. *Poly-Olbion,* which he had intended as his literary monument, had become an antiquarian curiosity.

Chapter Six
"that fine madnes": Folio of 1619

Poems

For Drayton, as for many literary figures in the English Renaissance, patronage meant more than money or protection; it signified literary and social recognition. In 1616, when Ben Jonson published the folio edition of his *Works,* he was claiming laureate achievement.[1] Drayton's publication of the 1619 folio collection of his early work and later folios in 1627 and 1630 represents a similar claim. The engraved portrait prefacing the 1619 folio pictures a stern-faced Drayton, crowned with a laurel wreath. For this collection he selected from his published work those poems that he wished to preserve and supplied authoritative texts for them.

Since scholars have uncritically accepted statements in Drayton's prefaces and dedications as facts, it is worth noting the inaccuracies in his 1619 dedication to Sir Walter Aston. Regarding the chronology of his poems, Drayton says that they are "works of that Mayden Reigne" and the "fruit of that Muse-nursing Season" (2).[2] Four of the poems in 1619 appeared after James's accession, but Drayton prefers to date their composition before "Hell had sent up her black Furies, that in every corner breathe their venome in the face of cleere Poesie" (2). Like many Jacobean writers and courtiers, Drayton looked back nostalgically to the "flowery *Tempe*" of Elizabeth's reign.[3] He identifies Aston as the only patron of his early work: "as it pleased you then to *Patronize,* as I singly set them forth: so now collected into this small Volume; I make the best Present, that my poore Abilitie is able to tender you" (2). Since Drayton's tragical complaints (1593–96), *Mortimeriados,* and *Englands Heroicall Epistles* were dedicated to Lucy, Countess of Bedford, he is clearly misrepresenting the facts. Moreover, he had no need to raise the issue of who patronized his poems when they first appeared. As late as 1619, he still wanted to insure that Lucy's patronage would be forgotten: "Nere be her name remembred more in rime" (Tillotson, 189).

Drayton's 1619 folio represents the fruition of many years of literary practice and reflection. For this collection he grouped his poems by genre and supplied a preface on each genre. The list below gives the works in the order

97

that they appear in the 1619 folio and notes parenthetically the dates of initial publication and of revisions, deletions, and additions in parentheses. *The Barons Warres,* Drayton's epic, appears as the first work in *Poems* (1619).

The Barons Warres (1603, 1605, 1619)

Englands Heroicall Epistles (1597, 1598, 1599, 1600, 1619)

Idea (1594, 1599, 1600, 1602, 1605, 1619)

Odes (1606, 1619)

The Legends	Of *Robert,* Duke of Normandie (1596, 1605, 1619)
	Matilda (1594, 1596, 1605, 1619)
	Peirs Gaveston (1593, 1595, 1596, 1605, 1619)
	Cromwell (1607, 1619)

The Owle (1604, 1619)

| Pastorals | *Eglogues* (1593, 1606, 1619) |
| | *Man in the Moone* (1606, 1619) |

Drayton's revisions have sometimes been dismissed as "tinkering," but he made no major substantive changes in *Englands Heroicall Epistles.* In 1619 he divided the epistles into verse paragraphs, but these poems were not subjected to the line-by-line revision that the legends received. He also retained a number of sonnets from *Ideas Mirrour* that were not revised.

From his years of experimentation and revision, Drayton had developed an appreciation of the interrelation of genre, conventions, and structure that fully informs *Poems* (1619). Of Drayton's revised works, the one that best suggests the quality of his critical perception is the final version of his sonnet sequence, the splendid *Idea* (1619).

Sonnets: *Idea*

Even in its initial version, Drayton's *Ideas Mirrour. Amours in Quatorzains* promises a reach that led Kathleen Tillotson to describe his work as sounding "almost as though Marlowe were writing sonnets," a comment seconded by C. S. Lewis and repeated by all of the critics who have assessed *Idea* in its various manifestations.[4] Comparison with Marlowe would have pleased Drayton. In his elegy to Henry Reynolds, "Of Poets and Poesie" (1627), he describes Marlowe as a poet who had in him "those brave translunary things" that the first poets had.[5]

> . . . his raptures were,
> All ayre, and fire, which made his verses cleere,
> For that fine madnes still he did retaine,
> Which rightly should possesse a Poets braine.
>   (107–10)

Idea (1619) represents Drayton's last and most successful attempt to convey "that fine madnes."

Drayton's final version of *Idea* brings together poetry written over a twenty-four-year period. He includes twenty sonnets dating from 1594, nineteen from 1599, seven from 1600, one from 1602, seven from 1605, and ten from 1619.[6] The composite nature of this sequence illustrates changes in taste and aesthetic principles between Elizabethan and Jacobean poetry.[7] Because Drayton continued revising and writing sonnets long after the vogue of Petrarchan poetry had waned, his revisions supplied Rosemond Tuve with a test for her argument that the imagery of metaphysical poetry was not a movement in the direction of T. S. Eliot and a poetics involving the multiplication of sensuous particulars, but an extension of Elizabethan rhetorical principles.[8] Her polemical apparatus, largely because her argument is now accepted, is less compelling after forty years than her astute judgments.

Acknowledging that Drayton's sonnets improved, Tuve attributes that improvement to "closer integration of form with poetic subject," shift to "a more satiric and mocking tone," and changes in "concept, syntax, and meter." Because of her interest in drawing the conclusion that no substantive change in aesthetics occurred between the sixteenth and seventeenth centuries, Tuve was reluctant to pursue the conclusion to be drawn from her own critical analysis. In spite of its composite bibliographical history, Drayton's *Idea* (1619) differs from *Ideas Mirrour* (1594) in quality and purpose.

Walter R. Davis has provocatively argued that *Idea* is a comic sequence, demonstrating that the poet will always be unsuccessful in his attempts to avoid conventionality.[9] Davis correctly observes that many of Drayton's poems begin unconventionally, only to conclude with the lover insisting on the worth of his mistress. This reversal of stance illustrates only one of many ways that Drayton explores convention. *Idea* examines the tension between poetic inspiration, "that fine madnes," and the conventions of the love sonnet as a literary form. The only genre not described in the 1619 folio is the sonnet sequence. Drayton offers no history or definition because the sequence itself acts as an analysis of the genre.

Drayton uses the conventions of the sonnet sequence as a framework within which he can examine and address the dilemmas of the poet. The poet in Drayton's sequence can be a devoted lover, but he can also be a changeable libertine. His rhetorical stance is intentionally flexible. He can play any number of roles in his attempt to express "Idea," the poetic and platonic Idea that can only be approximated in words. The themes of writing and evaluating are used throughout *Idea* to highlight the poet's problems in communicating his "fine madnes" to his mistress, his readers, and his critics.

In his prefatory sonnet Drayton introduces the topic of convention but mocks both the pretensions of his persona and the reader's expectations. We are told that in this sequence there will be no Petrarchan conventions. Instead of praising Idea as the "Queene of Poesie" and declaring his love for her as he had in *Ideas Mirrour*, Drayton's persona announces that his verse will focus on the poet's craft: "My Verse is the true image of my Mind" (9):

> Into these Loves, who but for Passion lookes,
> At this first sight, here let him lay them by,
> And seeke else-where, . . .
> No farre-fetch'd Sigh shall ever wound my Brest,
> Love from mine Eye a Teare shall never wring,
> Nor in Ah-mees my whyning Sonnets drest.
>   (1–3, 5–7)

Claiming to turn his back on Sidney and Spenser, he says that he will ignore the conventional poses of the Petrarchan lover. The sonneteer will suppress his sighs and tears, but, ironically, the suggestion that he must suppress his sighs reinforces our awareness of their existence.

Since in many sonnets Drayton's sonneteer sings passionately, not "fantastickly," the prefatory sonnet cannot be taken at face value. As this sonnet satirically suggests:

> . . . in all Humors sportively I range:
> My Muse is rightly of the English straine,
> That cannot long one Fashion intertaine.
>   (12–14)

Drayton's aim is to make his "verse" the "true image," not of the lover's heart, but of the poet's mind. The poet may cast himself in the role of a libertine whose mind is always changing, as in the prefatory sonnet, but he entertains more than "one Fashion." He may rework a hackneyed image, "My Heart the Anvile, where my Thoughts doe beate" (sonnet 40), or comment soberly upon contemporary history (sonnet 51). He may undercut his own persona and avowed purpose by inviting the reader to "read" over the "story" of his woes and "note" his sighs (sonnets 54 and 55). He sets out to give fresh life to outworn rhetorical figures, "Burn'd in a Sea of ice, and drown'd amidst a fire," in this instance, by extending paradox beyond its conventional reach (sonnet 62).

In sonnet 44 Drayton introduces the theme of carpe diem, but reverses conventional expectations by depicting the poet, rather than his mistress, as aging. The poet offers his unreceptive Petrarchan mistress a respite from oblivion in his "World-out-wearing Rimes" (7), but her "coy disdaine" insures that she is ignored in the last six lines of the sonnet. By implication she will also be forgotten by "ensuing Ages" (11). Paradoxically, the poet's unappreciated effort "to eternize" his mistress confers immortality on him by insuring the survival of his name. Inverting both carpe diem and the convention that the poet can immortalize his beloved, Drayton suggests that the despised poet-lover may triumph when his "Name shall mount upon Eternitie" (14).

Of all Drayton's sonnets, sonnet 61, which first appeared in the 1619 folio, is justly his most famous. In the opening line the poet-lover casually acknowledges the end of a love affair. Very much a man of the world, he invites his mistress to kiss before they part, but regrets his invitation in the second line:

> Since ther's no helpe, Come let us kisse and part,
> Nay, I have done: You get no more of Me,
> And I am glad, yea glad withall my heart,
> That thus so cleanly, I my Selfe can free
>
> (1–4)

In line three Drayton repeats "glad," using *ploce,* repetition of a word within a line, to signal that the speaker is affecting a nonchalance that he does not feel. The next quatrain intensifies the impression that the speaker is pretending indifference:

> Shake hands for ever, Cancell all our Vowes,
> And when We meet at any time againe,
> Be it not seene in either of our Browes,
> That We one jot of former Love reteyne
>
> (5–8)

The lover's suggestion that they shake hands, as though symbolically agreeing that there will be no hard feelings, is undermined by lines six through eight. If they are going to agree to part amicably, why does he place such stress on never acknowledging each other in the future? The intrusion of the colloquial word "jot," while it helps to create the impression of a conversation, harshly conveys the speaker's suppressed bitterness.

The sestet of sonnet 61 sharply differs in tone from the octet. Organizing these lines around the central image of Love's death, Drayton uses the traditional personifications of Petrarchan poetry to achieve a remarkably subtle shift in tone:

> Now at the last gaspe, of Loves latest Breath,
> When his Pulse fayling, Passion speechlesse lies,
> When Faith is kneeling by his bed of Death,
> And Innocence is closing up his Eyes,
> Now if thou would'st, when all have given him over,
> From Death to Life, thou might'st him yet recover.
>   (9–14)

The lover is deeply sincere in his regard for his mistress: Love, gasping for breath on his deathbed, is attended by Passion, but also by Faith and Innocence. The use of present participles, "fayling" (10), "kneeling" (11), and "closing" (12), draws out the climax, emphasizing that the love affair might be revived. To accentuate the indefiniteness of the parting Drayton uses conditional verbs in the couplet. Love might "recover" and their relationship continue.

The emotional energy of sonnet 61 is generated by the contrasting styles of the octet and sestet. In the first eight lines the speaker talks about events in the past and the future, masking the bitterness of his present feelings with a pose of indifference. If it were not for the octet, the stock Petrarchan personifications of the sestet would seem hackneyed and outworn. The juxtaposition renders the standard Petrarchan devices symbolic. Neither the acrimonious tone of the octet, nor the conventional Petrarchan personifications of the sestet betray the lover's feelings. The plea he makes in the couplet exposes his anguish, revitalizing the Petrarchan personifications of the sestet. This sonnet accomplishes in miniature Drayton's objective in the entire sonnet sequence. He wants to prove that conventions are meaningful, not to expose them satirically, as Walter Davis has suggested.

Drayton's ironic techniques in sonnet 61 illustrate how we are to read *Idea* (1619). In sonnet 6, also printed first in 1619, the poet-lover violates decorum by beginning satirically, even grimly:

> How many paltry, foolish, painted things,
> That now in Coaches trouble ev'ry Street,
> Shall be forgotten, whom no Poet sings,
> Ere they be well wrap'd in their winding Sheet?
>   (1–4)

By the conclusion of the poem the poet promises his mistress that her fame will endure: ". . . above the vulgar Throng, / Still to survive in my immortall Song" (14). C. S. Lewis selects the following lines from this sonnet as examples of "towering hyperbole":

> When nothing else remayneth of these dayes,
> And Queenes hereafter shall be glad to live
> Upon the Almes of thy superfluous prayse.
>   (6-8)

Singling out the line beginning, "And Queenes hereafter," Lewis claims that Drayton has surpassed even Shakespeare, establishing a "seamark beyond which poetry in that kind has never gone nor could go," adding that if Drayton "had never written another verse, these two would secure him that praise which is due to men who have done some one thing to perfection."[10] The differences in diction and tone between the first and second quatrains in sonnet 6 not only enhance the hyperbole, but also make the reader aware of the poet's artifice. His "song" and "his prayse" receive our attention.

In sonnet 24, first introduced in 1600, the poet is accused of not being sincerely in love because of the lightness of his tone:

> I heare some say, this Man is not in love:
> Who? can he love? a likely thing, they say;
> Reade but his Verse, and it will eas'ly prove.
>   (1-3)

The poet replies that because he "loosely trifle[s]," this does not invalidate his passion. Other men may cry out, but he laughs at Fortune "as in jest to die" (14). By pointing out that "censures" may mistake tone, he has suggested that the critic may misread sonnet 24 and, by implication, *Idea* as a whole. Sonnet 24 undercuts the pose that the sonneteer assumes in the prefatory sonnet, reinterpreting the "libertine," who sings "fantastickly"; Drayton's "personal" voice is itself an ironic construct.

He defends his originality in the comic sonnet 31, dating from 1599, by claiming to pay no attention to criticism. This pose is a typical one for the Petrarchan poet, but the selection of images turns the poem into an effective satire on high and low style and an exploration of decorum:

> Methinkes I see some crooked Mimicke jeere,
> And taxe my Muse with this fantasticke Grace,
> Turning my Papers, askes, What have we heere?
> Making withall some filthy Antike Face.
>   (1–4)

The imbedded question, "What have we heere," leads to an assertion of originality, "Think'st thou, my Wit shall keepe the pack-Horse Way" (7) that puns on "low invention" (8). Ironically, in the couplet Drayton shifts his stance and becomes not the conventional Petrarchan poet, but a poet whose own artistic claims are amusing but effective.

By the time that Drayton assembled *Idea* (1619), the conventions of the sonnet sequence that he, like many other less talented writers, had used in the 1590s as props for a set of poetic exercises seemed outworn. In spite of his having named his mistress and his muse "Idea," Drayton was not an intellectual poet. His insights came from working concretely with the material of poetry during his long apprenticeship as a sonneteer. His final version of *Idea* is different in quality from *Ideas Mirrour,* but it is also different in kind. In 1594 he asserted his originality and his independence from convention. By 1619 he was critically aware of convention and could explore and articulate the problems an artist faced in working in a conventional form.

This tension becomes the subject of sonnet 34, first printed in 1599:

> Marvell not, Love, though I thy Pow'r admire,
> Ravish'd a World beyond the farthest Thought,
> And knowing more then ever hath beene taught.
>   (1–3)

The poet knows more than he has been taught because he is inspired, "Ravish'd a World beyond the farthest Thought." His inspiration leads him to aim "at things exceeding all perfection" (6). Inspiration cannot be expressed in outworn conventions. Poetic conceits must be "bent" and invention "extended" to express the "marvell" of poetic inspiration:

> Marvell not, Love, though I thy power admire,
> Though my Conceit I further seem to bend
> Than possibly Invention can extend.
>
> (7–9)

In this sonnet, firmly grounded in Petrarchan conventions, Drayton gives unforgettable expression to an art that is "ravish'd a World beyond the farthest Thought." For *Idea* (1619) Drayton wrote, "Since ther's no helpe, Come let us kisse and part," a sonnet that illustrates the techniques used throughout his sequence. He included in the sequence those sonnets that singly and together expressed the tension between poetic inspiration, "that fine madnes," and literary convention.

Genre: The Ode and the Pastoral

Drayton's prefaces in *Poems* (1619) illustrate the theoretical understanding of genre that he gained from practice. As early as the preface to *Englands Heroicall Epistles* (1597), Drayton revealed a naive interest in genre. This interest matured as he experimented with new forms, such as the ode, and redefined established forms, such as the complaint. The 1619 prefaces merit critical attention because they shed light on early conceptions of genre.

Since John Southern's *Pandora* (1584) does not discuss the ode as a literary form, Drayton is credited with introducing this idea, and his odes, appearing in *Poemes Lyrick and pastorall* (1606), are the first to merit literary attention.[11] His major critical contribution, however, is his attempt to establish an English tradition for the ode. He does this tentatively, revealing his intention by allusions in his verse and by marginal glosses rather than by direct statement. In his preface on the ode (1606, 1619) he surveys classical kinds, identifying the Pindaric as "transcendently loftie," even more sublime than the epic poem (345). The Anacreonic ode will be "amorous, soft, and made for Chambers." The third kind, associated with Horace, is called "mixed." His comments on the relationship between genre and meter show that Drayton is pondering what metrical forms may be appropriate for the English ode: "the Ode is . . . a Song, moduled to the ancient Harpe, and neither too short-breathed, as hasting to the end, nor composed of the longest Verses, as unfit for the sudden Turnes and loftie Tricks" (345). To approximate in verse these "sudden Turnes" and "loftie Tricks," Drayton adapts "*Skelton's Ryme*" (95), as he acknowledges in "To Himselfe, and the Harpe." The Skeltonic furnishes Drayton with his native model.

By 1619 he has consciously identified a distinctly British background for the ode. In his dedicatory poem he associates his "Lyric Pieces, short, and few" with British bards:

> Th'old *British* Bards, upon their Harpes,
> For falling Flatts, and rising Sharpes,
>   That curiously were strung;
> To stirre their Youth to Warlike Rage,
> Or their wyld Furie to asswage,
>   In these loose Numbers sung.
>
>   (13–18)

The ode, appearing first in the 1619 edition, "To Himselfe, and the Harpe," asserts Drayton's intention to revive "th'old *Lyrick* kind" (5). He also experiments with the ballad, "with the old English Garbe," innovating in true Renaissance fashion by recovering a traditional form.

In 1619 Drayton added eight new odes and dropped two that had previously appeared in 1606. Six of the eight new odes are love lyrics, modeled on Anacreon rather than Pindar or Horace. It has been suggested by one critic that Drayton's models and subject matter changed in response to contemporary appreciation of "Cavalier" lyrics, but metaphysical influences have also been detected.[12] His odes reflect both influences. In "To his Coy Love" he takes a Cavalier stance, but his imagery evokes a disturbing sensuality. The texture of the new odes is still Skeltonic, but he has intensified the imagery and straightened out the syntax.

Drayton is also interested in the history of the pastoral and the conventions appropriate to it. His preface on the pastoral as a genre, first printed in 1619, reflects his increased interest in interpretation of literary texts. He assumes that the pastoral will be a fiction, not the realistic songs of shepherds, and that the work will be allegorical. Pastorals are "fained Dialogues, or other speeches in Verse, fathered upon Heardsmen" (517). He mentions that many pastorals contain references to actual people or events "shaddowed" in them:[13]

The subject of Pastorals, as the language of it ought to be poor, silly, & of the coursest Woofe in appearance. Neverthelesse, the most High, and most Noble Matters of the World may bee shaddowed in them, and for certaine sometimes are:

but he who hath almost nothing Pastorall in his Pastorals, but the name (which is my Case) deales more plainly, because *detracto velamine,* he speakes of most weightie things. (517)

Drayton's observations contain useful insights concerning Renaissance perceptions of allegory. If the meaning of a poem about shepherds is hidden in pastoral trappings, then it is more "pastoral" and more "allegorical." If the cloud of allegory is drawn aside and there is "nothing in the Pastoral but the name," then the work "deales more plainly." Drayton's comments exactly reverse our conceptions of symbolism and allegory—the clearer the precept the less allegorical the poem.

Defining a Genre: From Tragical Complaint to Legend

While Drayton's interest in defining the ode and the pastoral is noteworthy, the actual task of defining these genres cannot have been difficult. Both the ode and the pastoral were canonical forms because ample numbers of classical and continental models existed and because they could be defined with some precision. That was by no means true of the kind of poem that Drayton treated as a complaint in 1594, but later defined as a legend. His revisions of his tragical complaints in 1596, 1605, and 1619 illustrate the way in which he gradually defined a genre through practice and then worked out a theoretical definition to account for the result.

Drayton's tragical complaints, *Peirs Gaveston* (1593), *Matilda* (1594), and *Robert of Normandy* (1596), derived from two contradictory traditions: the didactic tradition associated with the *Mirror for Magistrates* and the decorative and erotic tradition associated with the Ovidian minor epic. When he revised his complaints in 1596, he was experimenting with the minor epic, and so his revisions further embellished poems that were already laden with decorative passages.

In 1605 he changed his aesthetic strategy. Nearly all of the embellishments introduced in 1596 were removed. Drayton deleted forty-nine stanzas from *Robert of Normandy* and compressed others, reducing the poem from 1,426 lines in 1596 to 945 lines in 1605. In 1605 all but one (372–78) of the stanzas added to *Matilda* in 1596 were removed. *Peirs Gaveston* went through a similar process of expansion in 1596 and reduction, by nearly two-thirds, in 1605. His pruning of the complaints shows that he was no longer inclined toward the effusive rhetorical display of the minor epic. Although he did not fully sort out the point of his revisions and their relation to genre until 1619, by 1605 Drayton had begun to conceive of a short historical poem with different conventions from those of the Ovidian minor epic or the earlier complaints in *Mirror for Magistrates*.

When he defines the legend as a genre for the first time in 1619, he derives the term etymologically from the Latin gerund, *legendum,* adding that it was "anciently used in an Ecclesiasticall sense, and restrained therein to things written in Prose, touching the Lives of Saints" (382). Spenser, he tells us, first translated the legend from prose to verse. He has forgotten Chaucer's *Legends of Good Women,* a work available in the 1532 edition of William Thynne.[14] He conceives of the legend as "a *Species* of an *Epick* or *Heroick Poeme.*" Shrugging off specifics, Drayton comments that to "particularize the Lawes of this Poeme, were to teach the making of a Poeme; a Worke for a Volume, not an Epistle. . . . it eminently describeth the act or acts of some one or other eminent Person; not with too much labour, compasse, or extension, but roundly rather, and by way of Briefe, or Compendium" (382). He regarded these brief lives of eminent people as furnishing moral lessons for his readers and supplies a moral for each of his legends. Regarding *Robert of Normandy,* he enigmatically says that this legend shows that misfortune can occur to the just, that "[e]vents are not the measure of Counsels, Gods pleasure over-swaying in all, for hidden Causes" (382). *Matilda,* as it would not be difficult to guess, illustrates the virtue of chastity. These are fairly transparent interpretations.

His morals for *Peirs Gaveston* and *Cromwell* reveal more about how Drayton wanted us to read the poems than about the poems themselves. His readings are surprisingly political. *Peirs Gaveston* offers a warning to the favorites of princes to use their influence with their royal patrons modestly. This might be a cautious warning to George Villiers, Duke of Buckingham, but the moral for *Cromwell* is a full-fledged sermon to the royal favorite. Drayton warns that a "new Mans fortune" may not be secure if dependent upon "a corrupt Prince, and Times": "in *Cromwell* thou hast the Example of a new Mans fortune, made great by Arts of Court, and reach of a Shrewd Wit, upon the advantages of a corrupt Prince, and Times; shewing, that nothing is certaine in newnesse, where the Creatures Fall may in some measure deliver the mortall Creator from the envie of his proper Acts, and Insolencies" (382). Significantly, the fall of Cromwell teaches us not to avoid overreaching ambition but to distrust kings. The "mortall Creator" may decide to sacrifice his creature if the "Creatures Fall" will make it possible for the "mortall Creator" to escape the blame for his own "Acts, and Insolencies." The morals that Drayton selects for both *Peirs Gaveston* and *Cromwell* emphasize secular politics over Christian ethics.

Drayton "reads" his own legends as his contemporaries had read his *Englands Heroicall Epistles.*

Matilda

In this legend the already-married King John tries to seduce Matilda, daughter of Lord Robert Fitzwalter. Faced with this threat to her honor, she retreats to a nunnery. John sends a messenger to offer her the choice between dishonor and death; Matilda chooses death. Daniel's *Complaint of Rosamund* (1592) had strongly influenced the 1594 version of *Matilda,* especially the descriptions of Matilda's beauty and Fitzwalter's lament over his daughter's death. When Drayton began to conceive of the legend as a literary kind with its own conventions, he redefined this story, as his 1619 preface indicates, in relation to the saint's life. In the 1594 text Matilda takes poison from the king's messenger and kills herself; in 1605 and 1619 the king's messenger forcibly poisons her.

By 1605, certainly by 1619, Drayton realized that if he wished this poem to serve as a secular "saint's life" or legend, then Matilda could not take her own life. He revised her death from suicide to murder so that the shape of the narrative would accord with his concept of genre. By 1619 Daniel's influence on Drayton has disappeared; the romantic elements in the earlier versions have been eliminated or subordinated to Drayton's new generic conception of the legend.

Robert of Normandy

William the Conqueror chose his second son William Rufus as his heir, but his oldest son Robert Curthose took Normandy by force and then joined Godfrey of Bouillon on the First Crusade. Robert left Normandy in the hands of Henry Beauclerc, his youngest brother. When William Rufus died, Henry seized both Normandy and England; he later imprisoned and blinded Robert upon his return from the Crusades. The story of Robert had already been told by Thomas Lodge. In 1591 he had published *Robert Second Duke of Normandy (Robin the Devil)* with a preface claiming that he had written the true life of Robert from antiquarian sources, but, in fact, he just recounted the usual legends.

Drayton used Holinshed's *Chronicles* as his primary source, but his glosses suggest that he also examined some of Holinshed's sources. Robert's character is largely Drayton's invention. He acknowledges that Tasso mentions Robert in *Gerusalemme Liberata,* but chides him for not relating his story:

O wherefore thou Great *Singer* of thy dayes,
Renowned *Tasso* in thy Noble Story,
Wert thou so slacke in this Great *Worthy's* prayse?
(792–94)

To remedy Tasso's omission, Drayton supplies an English hero for the story
of the liberation of Jerusalem. Drayton's Robert becomes an ideal Christian
military leader. Robert refuses the crown of Jerusalem because he scorns titles
and worldly glory. Drayton's chronicle sources attribute Robert's rejection of
the crown to his desire for the English crown (Holinshed) or to a slothful "fear
of endless labour" (William of Malmesbury) (Tillotson, 39).

Drayton frames *Robert of Normandy* in each of the three editions (1596,
1605, and 1619) with a medieval dream vision, a form used in the early
Mirror for Magistrates tradition. The poet falls asleep and dreams of a debate
between Fame and Fortune over the life and suffering of Robert. The significance of the relationship between the dream vision and the debate structure
has not been recognized. Drayton uses this debate structure to turn *Robert of
Normandy* into a commentary on the *Mirror for Magistrates* tradition. Fortune, the dominant force in the *Mirror* tradition, offers a *de casibus* explanation of Robert's misfortune. He is depicted as the hapless toy of fate. Fame
counters this medieval *de casibus* view of Robert's life. In Fame's view
Robert's character affects his fate; he is more than a plaything of Fortune.
Fame dwells on his heroism in Jerusalem; his life may come to a tragic conclusion, but the fame of his deeds will endure. As the dream vision frame suggests, the poet endorses Fame's version of Robert's life and insures that his
heroic deeds will be remembered. Although Drayton cut substantially from
every other part of this poem, he always retained every line of the dream vision. He used this frame to subordinate the medieval *de casibus* view of a
man's life, derived from chronicle history, to a Renaissance celebration of
character, triumphing over Fortune.

Robert of Normandy begins as the narrator falls asleep on the bank of
the Thames near London. In 1596 he suddenly hears the noise of trum-
pets, as when "great Beta [his name for Elizabeth] in her pompe wee see"
(52). In the 1619 version James is not specifically mentioned; when triumphal music sounds, we merely see "the Sov'raigne" (52) on his barge.
The poet awakens to the vision of a knight accompanied by two ladies.
Fame stands to Robert's right, wearing a golden gown embroidered with
the deeds of all the Worthies, her train carried by Time. Fortune like the
knight is blind; she wears "[t]orne Diadems and broken Scepter's" (107)

around her neck as a chain and carries bags of gold to throw to "Sots and arrant idiots" (112).

When Drayton revised the 1596 text, he deleted epithets and rhetorical decoration. In instances in which he retained a stanza from the 1596 edition, but revised it, he tightens and strengthens the syntax. Whenever Drayton makes substantive changes as he moves from 1596 to 1605 to 1619, the successive revisions depict a bleaker world. In 1596 Fame concludes her speech by defying "Times sacriligious rapine"; she will act as "A tributarie to eternitie" (377–78). In 1605 Drayton revises her conclusion to "The Rape of Time I carelessly defie" (377), but in 1619 that line becomes, "The Power of Kings I utterly defie." The monarch, the focus of political and cultural patronage, lacks the power to silence Fame. She no longer acts as "A tributarie to eternitie"; she concludes, "Nor am I aw'd by all their Tyrannie" (378). In 1619 "the Rape of Time" distresses Drayton less than the "Power of Kings" and "all their Tyrannie."

Drayton's critical interest in decorum leads him to sacrifice memorable images and fine lines if the result is improved clarity. In 1596 stanza 55 contains a number of vague images that are clarified in 1619. The first line in 1596 describes the "face of heaven" as containing Fame's "chronicles." In 1619 Drayton carefully revises this stanza to clarify the relationship between Fame and the constellations:

> The Brow of Heav'n my Monuments containe,
> (And is the mightie Register of Fame)
> Which there in fierie Characters remaine,
> The gorgeous Seeling of th'immortall Frame,
> The Constellations publishing my Name,
> Where my Memorials evermore abide,
> So by th'old Poets was I glorify'd.
>
> (344–51)

Drayton's allusion in line 351 to "old Poets" who glorified Fame was added in 1619. This allusion, like his symbolic use of the dream vision to frame the poem, suggests that the vision of the poet preserves a truth more lasting and compelling than historical chronicles. Fortune's power to inflict suffering ends with Robert's death; Fame has recorded his achievements, but it is the poet who "glorifies his fame" and insures a lasting record of his life.[15]

Chapter Seven
Folios of 1627 and 1630
The 1627 Folio

In 1627 Drayton published a folio collection under the title of the work appearing first in the volume, *The Battaile of Agincourt*. This 2,500-line poem concerns the English victory over the French in 1415. The next poem in the volume, *The Miseries of Queene Margarite*, versifies a chronicle of the War of the Roses. After these two poems on English history, Drayton includes *Nimphidia, the Court of Fayrie, The Quest of Cynthia*, and *The Shepheards Sirena*. These richly imaginative late pastorals elaborate the "fairy" motif Drayton had used earlier in his pastoral eclogue on the courtship of Dowsabell. They resemble Shakespeare's late romances and the fairy poetry of Robert Herrick. The pastorals are followed by *The Moone-Calfe*, a misanthropic poem in which the "old wives' tale" turns into satire and nightmare. This remarkably heterogeneous collection concludes with a series of occasional poems, funeral elegies, and verse epistles that Drayton calls *Elegies*.[1] He uses the term *elegy* for poems that we would be likely to consider verse epistles because he associated the *epistle* with the Ovidian epistle and so with fictional letters, like those he had invented in *Englands Heroicall Epistles*.

Although no poem in the 1627 folio closely resembles any of Drayton's previous work, that does not mean these poems are all new. Two of the funeral *Elegies* in the 1627 folio can be dated more than ten years earlier, "Upon the Three Sonnes of the Lord Sheffield" (December 1614) and "An Elegie Upon the Death of the Lady Penelope Clifton" (26 October 1613). An allusion to the possibility that the Irish might drive out the Earl of Tyrone in *The Moon-Calfe* suggests that a much earlier version of this poem may have existed. Hugh, Earl of Tyrone, fled from Ireland in 1607 and died in 1616. Most of the allusions in the *Elegies* that can be dated refer to events occurring between 1618 and 1622, but from what we know of Drayton's literary practice, he probably revised any poems that did not satisfy his critical standards before their publication in 1627.

Caroline Historical Epic and Chronicle: *The Battle of Agincourt*

Bernard Newdigate suggested that *The Battaile of Agincourt* was a patriotic poem inspired by Buckingham's 1627 expedition to relieve the French Protestants in La Rochelle (Newdigate, 210). If Drayton, at long last, agreed with government policy, he had every reason to connect his celebration of English military prowess with the La Rochelle expedition, but no parallels are made between Agincourt and La Rochelle. The dating evidence alone renders a connection unlikely.[2] The expedition to La Rochelle was not publicized until the winter of 1627, and *The Battaile of Agincourt* was registered on 16 April 1627. This unpopular expedition was difficult to finance, and so Buckingham's fleet did not actually leave England until the end of June 1627, after *The Battaile of Agincourt* was in print.

The Battaile of Agincourt is dedicated to the noble British gentlemen who retain the courage of their ancestors and who at the same time respect poetry: "who in these declining times, have yet . . . that sprightly fire, of your couragious Ancestors; . . . and who out of the vertue of your mindes, love and cherish neglected Poesie, the delight of Blessed Soules, and the language of Angels" (2*). Rather than sounding a new note of patriotism, Drayton reiterates his dissatisfaction with a society in which *The Battaile of Agincourt,* like *Poly-Olbion,* may not find a responsive audience. He presented a copy of *The Battaile of Agincourt* to Sir Henry Willoughby, a distinguished military leader, with a handwritten dedication addressing him as "one of the selected Patrons of thes my latest Poemes" (Tillotson, 194). Drayton's preface to the 1627 collection facilitated his distributing a series of presentation copies to prospective patrons.

Political attitudes in Parliament shifted radically after Charles's accession in 1625. In the context in which it appeared Drayton's *Battaile of Agincourt* must have seemed ironic. Although in 1621 Parliament had been adamant about the need to support James's daughter and son-in-law in recovering the Palatinate, Parliament was far from sanguine about Buckingham's administration of the navy. In Charles's first Parliament in 1625, Buckingham was strongly criticized for the mismanagement of the joint French and English expedition led by Count Ernst von Mansfield. In 1626 Parliament tried to impeach Buckingham to punish him for the failure of the Cadiz expedition in 1625. Furthermore, concessions made to English Catholics to secure Charles's French marriage were extremely unpopular.

England had been humiliated on the sea and at the negotiating table. A poem celebrating the historic English victory over the French in 1415 served in 1627 only to underscore England's repeated military and diplomatic defeats. *The Battaile of Agincourt* stands first in a collection that concludes with Drayton's *Elegies*. The *Elegies* include poems that criticize James's foreign policy and bitterly attack his abridgment of liberty. Patriotism is not always positive; Drayton's celebration of England's past military triumph served as a foil to highlight inept Stuart administration and naval expeditions.[3]

The Battaile of Agincourt, not to be confused with Drayton's earlier ode entitled the "Ballad of Agincourt" (1606, 1619), is the finest historical narrative that he produced in his long career. In his prefatory poem Jonson compares Drayton's *The Barons Warres* (1603, 1619) with Lucan and *The Battaile of Agincourt* (1627) with Homer. This generous hyperbole points to a new departure in Drayton's historical verse. *The Battaile of Agincourt* does not focus on the adventures of a central hero, for example, Henry V. In *The Barons Warres* and his *Legends* Drayton engages in individual portraiture, but *The Battaile of Agincourt* deals broadly with men and events. Because of this sweeping approach to history, this poem achieves a unity of action uncharacteristic of Drayton's earlier historical poetry.[4] In *The Battaile of Agincourt* he shows that he understands Jonson's insight that "the Action of one man" may be an episode in a story; to have unity requires that the entire narrative have a focus.[5] Drayton organizes his poem around one action, the encounter of the English and the French at Agincourt.

The poem begins with a brief description of how the clergy, concerned about criticism by reformers like John Wyclif, introduced the French expedition as a means of diverting attention away from church reform.[6] The poem extends from the Parliament of Leicester, in which the English claim to the throne of France is revived, through the English victory at Agincourt, ending somewhat abruptly as Henry and his army march toward Calais, leaving the French to mourn their losses.

Drayton's weak imitations of specific epic devices, such as the catalog of ships borrowed from the *Iliad,* illustrate the impossibility of achieving an epic by imitating details in Homer or Vergil. In spite of these awkward and mechanical imitations, Drayton approximates a Homeric vision. *The Battaile of Agincourt* celebrates heroism and pays tribute to glory, but war is evaluated within the context of a broader perspective on human experience. The battle scenes, which his contemporaries praised, vividly depict the mutual slaughter of English and French soldiers: ". . . each body seem'd but as a sheath / To put their swords in, to the Hilts in gore" (1,653–54). Even in the midst of scenes such as these, he supplies epic similes that, like those of Homer, remove us from the immediacy of blood lust:

> Looke how you see a field of standing Corne,
> When some strong winde in Summer haps to blowe,
> At the full height, and ready to be shorne,
> Rising in waves, how it doth come and goe
> Forward and backward, so the crowds are borne.
>
> (1,657–61)

The ripple of the wind through standing corn reminds us that grain must be harvested. Epic similes parallel events in battle with natural phenomena—a field of corn, a flock of crows, a rolling tide. These similes serve as uncanny reminders that war is unnatural. Nature broods over the battlefield in *The Battaile of Agincourt*.

Drayton's celebration of English valor is not a partisan account of England's victory over France. Perhaps he learned from Homer's treatment of the noble Hector, because throughout *The Battaile of Agincourt* he acknowledges French heroism. To be sure, he apologizes for the English by suggesting that the killing of French prisoners of war is justified because the French would have treated the English in the same way. The French, however, have their heroes. Anthony, Duke of Brabant, is outraged by the defection of cowardly French soldiers and announces that he will oppose the English army without support (2,049–80). Likewise, the Duke of Alençon bravely attacks King Henry; when defeated, he asks to be ransomed, but before Henry can save him, he is overwhelmed by "rude Souldiers" who "that brave Duke into small peeces cut" (1,918, 1,920). In this episode, the aging Drayton, who had resented class distinctions as a young man, supports chivalric values against the threat of "rude" soldiers.

The militaristic thrust of his *Battaile of Agincourt* can be overstated. He never lets us lose sight of the cost of war. We are reminded that war causes human suffering and fosters greed and cruelty. Henry V tells his men not to harm those who are defenseless, the aged, maimed, and religious, but when the battle begins, an elderly man and his grandchild are killed by chance as are a newborn baby and its mother (785–800). Drayton describes the insults and indignities suffered by the defeated French (2,329–52). He also juxtaposes the glory of English heroism with descriptions of English soldiers looting the fallen French (2,465–504). He dramatizes the glamor of war, but does not ignore its brutality. He vividly offers distasteful portraits of the maimed:

> Slaughter is now desected to the full,
> Here from their backs their batter'd Armors fall,
> Here a sleft shoulder, there a cloven scull,
> There hang his eyes out beaten with a mall,
> Untill the edges of their Bills growe dull.
>
> (2,225–29)

The Battaile of Agincourt offers a panoramic view of war in which men behave with heroism and cowardice, humanity and cruelty. The English triumph does not overshadow the human price of victory.

Drayton's stance is by no means objective, but neither is it mindlessly patriotic. The English make war upon France to regain ancient glory, but their motives are not pure. The clergy who bring up the English claim to the French throne do so out of self-interest; English merchants support the war because they hope for new markets. Drayton's results may not be Homeric, but he has traveled a long way from the *Mirrour for Magistrates*.

The Miseries of Queene Margarite   The impersonal descriptive power that Drayton achieved in *The Battaile of Agincourt* did not work as effectively in *The Miseries of Queene Margarite*. He closely follows Holinshed's factual summary of the War of the Roses, but his point of view is so objective that neither side achieves either interest or moral ascendancy. In *Englands Heroicall Epistles* Drayton's annotations indicated that he viewed the York claim as stronger than that of the Lancastrians. The chroniclers Edward Hall, author of *The Union of the Noble and Illustre Fameles of Lancastre and York*, and Raphael Hollinshed, author of *The Chronicles of England, Scotland, and Ireland*, shared a Yorkist bias against Queen Margaret. Drayton's contemporary, the cartographer and historian John Speed, exhibits a Lancastrian bias in *Theatre of the Empire of Great Britaine* and *Historie of Great Britaine*. Drayton's opinion that the York claim to the throne was superior does not affect his characterization of Queen Margaret. He uses her suffering as a focal point for the narrative, but Margaret as a human figure remains so remote that her pathetic end becomes only one more event in a chronicle. When Drayton's panoramic vision failed, he lapsed into versified history.

Late Pastorals   Drayton's late pastorals demonstrate that the author of *Poly-Olbion* had the literary range to have succeeded as a court poet. He may have lacked the opportunity, or the inclination, to try his hand at a court entertainment, but it was fully within his capacity to have offered graceful lyrics in an imaginative context. One of his late pastorals, *Nimphidia, the*

Court of Fayrie, was adapted as a pantomime and successfully performed at Drury Lane in the eighteenth century (Tillotson, 202).

The three pastorals that appear in the 1627 folio, *Nimphidia, The Quest of Cynthia,* and *The Shepheards Sirena,* summon up the golden world of the imagination.[7] In his *Defence of Poetry* Sir Philip Sidney described this world in his well-known comparison between art and nature: "Nature never set forth the earth in so rich tapestry as divers poets have done; . . . Her world is brazen, the poets only deliver a golden."[8] Even in the golden world of his late pastorals in which art fulfills the promise of nature, Drayton allows irony to intrude on poetic fancy. *The Quest of Cynthia* begins with unpleasant reality and the pastoral world of *The Shepheards Sirena* is threatened by attacks from outside.

Nimphidia, the Court of Fayrie   As a means of alerting the reader to the literary background of *Nimphidia,* Drayton lists his predecessors as Chaucer, in his tale of Sir Thopas; Rabelais, in his story of the giants; and himself, in his story of Dowsabell in the fourth eclogue of his pastorals. Warren W. Wooden has suggested that *Nimphidia* may have been especially attractive to children and even intended as a poem that would attract a very broad, even youthful audience.[9] He may be correct, but *Nimphidia* is still a carefully wrought mock epic with deliberate literary allusions to Cervantes and Ariosto that children would be unlikely to perceive.

King Oberon accurately suspects that Queen Mab has become too fond of Pigwiggen. He becomes insanely jealous, more so than Orlando in Ariosto's *Orlando Furioso,* more distraught even than the classical heroes Ajax and Hercules. Drayton uses these epic comparisons artfully, but perhaps his greatest triumph is in exploiting the humorous potential of the diminutive size of the fairies. Armed with an acorn shell, Oberon mistakes a wasp for Pigwiggen and a glowworm for a devil because it carries a light in its tail. Hearing of Oberon's wrath, Queen Mab and her attendant fairies hurry away, finally taking shelter in a nutshell. At the end of the poem all of the male principals, Oberon, Tomalin, Pigwiggen, and Tom Thum, are persuaded to drink the water from Lethe. Oberon forgets his mad jealousy while Pigwiggen forgets his infatuation with the queen. Queen Mab and her fairies smile "closely" at each other, and then everyone returns to the fairy court for a feast. Magic cools passion.

Even *Nimphidia,* the lightest of Drayton's poems and a masterpiece of its kind, does not take place in a world without flaws. The setting is a fairy court where adultery is taken lightly, where pride and passion seem to rule. The mechanical and magical solution to violent passion is a draught of Lethe, the

water of forgetfulness. Lethe erases memories and so resolves the problems of
the fairies, but the very improbability of such an ending underscores the dis-
parity between the fairy kingdom and our world.

The Quest of Cynthia   Thematically linked to *Endimion and
Phoebe* (1595) and *The Man in the Moone* (1606, 1619), *The Quest of
Cynthia* is related to the myth in which Endymion falls in love with the
moon. Easily the most romantic of Drayton's poems, *The Quest of Cynthia*
has two parts: a description of the poet's quest for Cynthia, developed as an
encomium of her charms, and a description of the joy the poet experiences
when united with her.

The poet leaves behind "a den of mere dispight . . . Where onely villany is
wit, / And Divels onely thrive" (179–80) and enters the realm of Cynthia
"[s]uch as the golden world first sawe, / Most innocent and free" (183–84).
The solace that the poet experiences with Cynthia, a deity who embodies his
art, is held in defiance of the outside world. The poem concludes:

> By *Cynthia* thus doe I subsist,
>   On earth Heauens onely pride,
> Let her be mine, and let who list,
>   Take all the world beside.
>   (229–32)

Although the poet has claimed Cynthia and entered the golden world, he remains conscious of that other world from which his art is an escape. Poetry or
art as an end in itself remains an untenable compromise for Drayton, but in
this poem he comes closest to embodying a romantic escape from a world
that has ignored his public voice.

The Shepheards Sirena   In *The Shepheards Sirena* an unhappy
poet-shepherd is separated from his beloved Sirena and unsure of whether
he should follow her. This pretty but slight pastoral has generated an extraordinary amount of topical interpretation. A possible internal reference
to the Trent river led to the identification of Sirena as Mary Curzon, daughter of Sir George Curzon, owner of Croxall (Tillotson, 208; Newdigate,
211–14). This identification, pursued at length, has prompted a number
of wide-ranging interpretations of the poem's conclusion. In the concluding lines a shepherd tells the hero Dorilius that he must give up his sorrow
over Sirena and attend to the immediate needs of his flock. He warns him
that "Rougish Swinheards" plan to bring their swine into his fields and root

up the pasture. The swineherds are being encouraged by Olcon (Drayton's name for James):

> Angry *Olcon* sets them on,
> And against us part doth take
> Ever since he was out-gone,
> Offring Rymes with us to make.
>   (368–71)

The swineherds have been interpreted both as the "sons of Ben Jonson" and as the "school of Donne," but this poem seems far too slender a reed upon which to play specific topical references.[10] The poem ends inconclusively. Dorilius is told by his shepherd friend that they have dogs who will assist in defending their pastoral lands, but we are not sure if Dorilius joins the effort to defend the golden world from assault.

The Shepheards Sirena brings together themes and images that increasingly obsessed Drayton. His isolation from the court, the principal source of the kind of recognition he sought, intensified his interest in the contemporary literary scene. In his commendatory poem for William Browne's *Britannia's Pastorals* (1613), he uses imagery that is repeated in *The Shepheards Sirena:*

> . . . to the *Muses* once so sacred, Downes,
> As no rude foote might there presume to stand:
> (Now made the way of the unworthiest Clownes,
> Dig'd and plow'd up with each unhallowed hand).
>   (1:502)

Drayton expected serious poets to undertake great poetic enterprises; those who angled for preferment betrayed his conception of the poet as an Orphic bard who ought to contribute to culture. Poets who failed to espouse Drayton's view of the poet's social responsibility figured in his work as swineherds, threatening to defile the springs of the Muses, or rustic clowns, likely to root up the traditions that allowed poetry to flower. The imagery in *The Shepheards Sirena* illustrates his conviction that poetry was threatened by a reward system that ignored heroic enterprise undertaken by the sword or the pen.

The Moone-Calfe   Drayton's *The Moone-Calfe* (1627) may have been written as early as 1607, but its themes connect this poem with Drayton's darkest elegies. As the organizing motif for *The Moone-Calfe,* he

uses several variations on the "the world upside down." In his elegy addressed
to William Browne he supplies what might be an epigraph for *The
Moone-Calfe:*

> All arsey varsey, nothing is it's owne,
> But to our proverbe, all turnd upside downe;
> To doe in time, is to doe out of season,
> And that speeds best, thats done the farth's from reason.
>
> (53–56)

The Moone-Calfe divides into two parts linked principally by "our proverbe,
all turnd upside downe" (54) and an atmosphere of brooding sexuality in
which confused gender roles symbolize moral perversion.

The first part of *The Moone-Calfe* opens with a personification of the
World as pregnant with the monstrous moon-calf, the fruit of an unholy
union between the World and the Devil. This part of the poem employs the
kind of hyperbole that Donne uses in *An Anatomy of the World,* the first of his
two *Anniversaries* on Elizabeth Drury. As Kathleen Tillotson has observed,
The Moone-Calfe is important as an "extreme statement of the misanthropy
which mutters in the background of all Drayton's poems after 1603"
(Tillotson, 210). His brooding rage culminates in the image of the World as
a "luxurious Whore" (454). Lamenting that his time lacks the freedom of the
brave Romans, Drayton imagines the mutilation of the "World as Whore"
with wires and cords:

> With Wyer and Whipcord yee should see her payde,
> Till the luxurious Whore should be afrayde
> Of prostitution, and such lashes given,
> To make her blood spirt in the face of Heaven.
>
> (453–56)

The spurting blood will serve to remind men ambitious for preferment that
plagues will be visited upon those who prostitute themselves. The brutality
of the image underscores Drayton's rage against a society bent on substitut-
ing expediency for moral aspiration.

The foreboding aura of dark magic established in the first part of *The
Moone-Calfe* continues in the second. Beginning at line 575 four exempla are
related by old wives who assist Hecate, the goddess of witches, and the Furies
at the birth of the moon-calf. These exempla contain elements of the beast
fable and proverbial folklore. We are first introduced to a land filled with

people rendered irrational by a mysterious hurricane; their madness makes them refuse to listen to good advice when they hear it. No less mysterious in the second tale is a magic island that moves around like a boat. The witch and ape, figuratively greed and ambition, are only vanquished by spirits of their likenesses. The third tale relates the story of two men, one of whom voluntarily becomes a werewolf while another is metamorphosed into an ass. The lowly ass exposes the werewolf's identity, suggesting that truth can be told by the humble. The last tale depicts beasts who act like men; starving cattle plunder a rich field until driven out; the pasture is destroyed and the cattle are imprisoned. There is more than a hint in this tale that poverty breeds revolt, but the revolt of the cattle leaves them worse off than before.

The Moone-Calfe expresses the deep disillusionment that Drayton felt near the end of his career. His despair over political corruption and the decay of learning led him to feel as though he were observing the decline of humane letters. In *The Owle* Drayton attacked a society in need of reform, but in 1604 he never doubted that reform was possible. By 1627, when he published *The Moone-Calfe,* he had lost even that confidence. The tradition of service to the state by informed and disinterested public servants had been eroded by a patronage system that rewarded self-interested opportunists. *The Moone-Calfe* satirizes the abuses of a society that lacks the will to reform itself.

The Elegies   Drayton included twelve elegies in the 1627 folio: five funeral elegies and seven Horatian verse epistles. All five of the funeral elegies and the occasional epistles, "Of his Ladies Not Comming to London" and "Upon the Noble Lady Astons Departure for Spain," adopt the conceited rhetoric of courtly compliment. Of these elegies, the most successful are the funeral elegies written upon the deaths of Lady Penelope Clifton and his "Incomparable Friend, Sir Henry Raynsford." In the latter poem Drayton dwells upon his own loss and praises Sir Henry as the best of friends. These poems show that Drayton could employ the hyperbole and witty conceits characteristic of seventeenth-century occasional verse.

His other elegies echo the despair of *The Moone-Calfe,* but their mature, deliberative style distinguishes them from that dark satire. The tone of these epistles ranges from the analytical evaluation of the literary canon offered in "To Henery Reynolds, Of Poets and Poesie," to the jeremiad delivered in "To My Noble Friend Master William Browne, of the evil time," to the stoic consolation offered in "To the Noble Lady, The Lady I. S., of worldly crosses."

The elegies addressed to "Master George Sandys, Treasurer for the English Colony in Virginia" and to "Master William Jeffreys, Chaplaine to the Lord Ambassadour in Spaine" specifically allude to the proclamations prohibiting discussion of state matters, foreign and domestic, issued on 24 December 1620 and reissued on 4 August 1621. The House of Commons protested these proclamations on the grounds that they abridged the "ancient Liberty of Parliamentary Actions and Discourse."[11] In 1624 yet another royal proclamation prohibited importing or printing any book on religion or state affairs without prior approval, and in 1626 another royal proclamation was issued forbidding all writing on controversial matters in religion.

The suppression of liberty of speech and the censorship of the press disturbed Drayton. In the elegy addressed "To Master George Sandys, Treasurer for the English Colony in Virginia," he says that other men "make it their hourely theame" to discuss the Palatinate, but that he dares not speak:

> To other men, although these things be free,
> Yet (George) they must be misteries to mee.
> I scarce dare praise a vertuous friend that's dead,
> Lest for my lines he should be censured.
> (15–18)

He encourages Sandys to complete his translation of Ovid's *Metamorphoses*. Poetry has been exiled from England to wander homeless, but perhaps Sandys can entice her to take up residence in Virginia.

Drayton regards himself as a prophet-poet whose countrymen refuse to heed him, just as the Jews ignored the warnings of Isaiah, Ezekiel, and Jeremiah (59–64). He envisions the onset of a darker age than the Middle Ages in which heroic verse will be ignored in favor of "[b]ase Balatry" (79). He alludes to the decline of classical Greece, dominated in his day by the Turks. In spite of Drayton's gloom, he never becomes apocalyptic. Even though he is convinced that "blind Gothish Barbarisme" will triumph during his age, he imagines a renaissance:

> . . . insuing ages shall,
> Raise her againe, who now is in her fall;
> And out of dust reduce our scattered rimes,
> Th'rejected jewels of these slothfull times.
> (85–88)

That future times may retrieve "th'rejected jewels of these slothful times" affords some consolation. Repeatedly, in the *Elegies*, Drayton marshals stoic resolution as a means of coping with his own dark time:

> *Apollo*'s brood must be couragious still,
> Let Pies, and Dawes, sit dumb before their death,
> Onely the Swan sings at the parting breath.
>
> (34–36)

In large part because he persevered in the Herculean labor of writing *Poly-Olbion,* his somewhat self-pitying image of himself as a poet under siege, trying to write verse in an unsatisfactory age, remains compelling.

In his elegy addressed "To Master William Browne, of the evill time," he echoes Gloucester's suggestion in *King Lear* that "those all-framing powers above" made man not out of love, "but only as a thing, / To make them sport with" (43–44). Dismayed that those who have never engaged in any worthy enterprise receive preferment, Drayton describes these favorites as base beggars:

> This Drone yet never brave attempt that dar'd,
> Yet dares be knighted, and from thence dares grow
> To any title Empire can bestow.
>
> (58–60)

His description of a "new man" so aptly summarizes the career of Buckingham that it is noteworthy that Drayton published this elegy in 1627 before Buckingham's assassination in 1628.

To account for the "evil time" in which he finds himself, Drayton offers an inversion of the classical myth of Deucalion and Pyrrha. When the gods flood the world to destroy evil men, Deucalion and Pyrrha are saved by their virtue. The gods enable them to replenish the earth with people by throwing stones over their shoulders. In Drayton's version, the devil swarms into the clouds and takes a purgative, voiding out of his backside a ribald crew of rascals. Just as the gods turned stones into men, the devil has turned his vile purge into beasts who have spread over England: "Owners of titles from an obscure name" (76).

In the elegy addressed "To Master William Jeffreys, the Chaplaine to the Lord Ambassadour in Spaine," Drayton does not mention his former patron, Sir Walter Aston. Allusions to the proclamations forbidding discussion of matters of state indicate that this poem was written in 1621 or 1622, when he was also battling with printers and booksellers over printing the second part of *Poly-Olbion.* In this poem he offers an astute analysis of the tone of his *Elegies.*

In my conceipt, friend, thou didst never see
A righter Madman then thou hast of me,
For now as *Elegiack* I bewaile
These poore base times; then suddainely I raile
And am *Satirick,* not that I inforce
My selfe to be so, but even as remorse,
Or hate, in the proud fulnesse of their hight
Master my fancy, just so doe I write.

                                            (87–94)

Since this elegy, like those addressed to George Sandys and William Browne, concerns Drayton's role as a poet, ignored by what he perceived as his audience, it is suggestive that he mentions that "remorse" as well as "hate" can overpower his elegiac intentions. He may at times have regretted his independence and still longed for the laureate recognition that he felt was the just reward of his commitment to the muse.

The 1630 Folio

In his 1630 folio collection Drayton included *The Muses Elizium* and three divine poems: *Noahs Floud, Moses His Birth and Miracles,* and *David and Goliah.* Although the collection is dedicated to Edward Sackville, Earl of Dorset, a second dedication "consecrates" (326) the divine poems to Mary, Countess of Dorset. The Earl of Dorset had patronized both Donne and Jonson, and Drayton's allusion to having received the earl's "Bounties" (246) suggests that he may have received a pension from the earl or the countess.[12] That is probably the explanation for Drayton's statement that the earl's favors have made Drayton one of his "family"; he adds, "I become happy in the title to be called *Yours*" (246). In this last of his dedications Drayton remains as independent as ever: "I have often adventured upon desperate untrodden wayes, which hath drawn some severe censures, upon many of my Labours, but that neyther hath nor can ever trouble me" (246). His use of the word "desperate" makes it difficult to assume that he was referring merely to literary innovation. *Poly-Olbion* had not been well received, but long before the appearance of his Herculean labor, Drayton had asserted his independence. The evidence is inconclusive, but it seems unlikely that after years of isolation from the court under James, Drayton would have become Dorset's client and joined the ranks of Caroline court poets.

The Muses Elizium   Drayton's last pastoral, *The Muses Elizium,*
has as its subtitle the statement, "Lately discovered, by a new way over
Parnassus," the mountain sacred to Apollo and the Muses. *The Muses
Elizium* includes a poetic preface entitled, "The Description of Elyzium," and
ten poems that Drayton calls "nimphalls." He coined the term *nymphal* in
Poly-Olbion, song 20 (4) where it is glossed as a "meeting or Feast of
Nymphs." Beginning with C. S. Lewis's comment that *The Muses Elizium* is
about, "if anything, Scaliger's and Sidney's *naturam alterum,*" nearly all critical commentary has agreed that the poem portrays the world of the imagination.[13] In "The Description of Elyzium" Drayton suggests the idealized
pastoral world of Elysium:

> There in perpetuall Summers shade,
> *Apolloes* Prophets sit
> Among the flowres that never fade,
> But flowrish like their wit.
>
> (85–88)

Elysium is the "Poets Paradice" (101), a realm in which art has achieved an
ideal, a golden world in which human nature approximates the perfection
of the idealized landscape. This untroubled, festively joyous world contrasts
to Felicia, a land ironically named "happy." In Elysium, Venus has the form
of a beautiful goddess, but in Felicia she is misshapen. In Felicia, the actual
world of seventeenth-century England, Venus is always engaged in com-
mercial activity. When the Elysian nymphs see her in Nymphal 7, she is
first disguised as an old witch and then as a peddler, selling charms and cos-
metics (56–88, 96–116). Residents of Elysium may visit Felicia, but the
only Felician allowed to visit Elysium is the weary Satyr, a poet-satirist,
whom the Muses favor because of his truthful "plainesse" (Nymphal
10.34). Drayton puns on satire and satyr, an uncouth mythical figure with
hooves instead of feet. In this late pastoral he abandons the pastoral name
Rowland, which he had used in his 1593 and 1606 pastorals; here, the old
Satyr functions as his persona.

That Drayton introduces a satire on England into a poem celebrating the
Elysium of the Muses warrants more attention than it has received.[14] He
could have written two poems, a pastoral celebrating the golden world of the
imagination and a satire depicting seventeenth-century England as an unhappy and unnatural land, but he deliberately chose to combine these two
distinct themes.

Significantly, Felicia is a Latin equivalent of the Greek pun used to render

the title "Poly-Olbion" as "happy Albion."[15] *The Muses Elizium* is Drayton's
last critical statement on the craft of poetry. He selects the name Felicia for
England, ironically portraying it as an unhappy isle because he intends *The
Muses Elizium* to serve as a commentary on *Poly-Olbion,* his poetic memorial.
Elysium, the "Muses onely bower of blisse" (103), and the actual world of
Felicia are no longer connected; poetry cannot bridge the gap between its
ideal world and the actual world of men. The *bonae litterae,* which taught
men how to live in society, have become unfashionable. The only direction
left for poetry, Drayton suggests, is to create its own romantic world, a self-
contained "golden world."

Drayton's old Satyr functions as a symbol of the future of the poet as well
as Drayton's persona. In *Poly-Olbion* he had celebrated the poet as an
Orpheus who could entice men to institute ceremonies and to lead a "civil"
life, as a figure who preserved culture. In *The Muses Elizium* the Orphic bard
of *Poly-Olbion* has metamorphosed into the figure of the lonely old Satyr.
Painfully and poignantly *The Muses Elizium* retracts Drayton's faith in the
public mission of the poet, burying the aspirations that led him to persevere
in writing *Poly-Olbion.*

His ideals have become tarnished just as the "once faire Felicia" has
been despoiled:

> Once faire *Felicia,* but now quite defac'd,
> Those Braveries gone wherein she did abound,
> With dainty Groves, when she was highly grac'd
> With goodly Oake, Ashe, Elme, and Beeches croun'd.
> (85–88)

The golden age of "faire Felicia" is irrevocably lost, just as Drayton's kind of
poetry has lost its audience.

The old Satyr depicts a people who, ignorant of their own history, have become contemptuous of the poetry that gave voice to their heroic ideals. They
have even turned upon the land and begun to deface and ravage its beauty.
The plundering of the forests prompts the Satyr, like an Old Testament
prophet, to denounce and prophesy "plagues . . . shortly to come" upon
"these viprous monsters":

> This cruell kinde thus Viper-like devoure
> That fruitfull soyle which them too fully fed;
> The earth doth curse the Age, and every houre
> Againe, that it these viprous monsters bred.

> I seeing the plagues that shortly are to come
> Upon this people cleerely them forsooke.
> (117–22)

No critic has read *The Muses Elizium* as Drayton wrote it. We have preferred to believe that Michael Drayton, the old Satyr, forgot about England, while he dreamed in Elysium, but Drayton does not escape into the "golden world." He was nourished within a humanist tradition that would have regarded "romanticism" as escapist, if not immoral. The Orphic bard, the civilizer, cannot escape into a world in which poetry becomes an end in itself. Satire is preferable; that is why Drayton uses the old Satyr as his persona. Art may survive in Elysium, but it will be an art cut off from the actual world in which men govern, wage war, and conduct their affairs.

The last two lines of *The Muses Elizium* juxtapose "that vile nation" with its past "glorious age," not nostalgically, but bitterly, prophesying that Felicia will become a captive nation. These lines glance back at Drayton's celebration of England's triumph over France in *The Battaile of Agincourt* (1627). This allusion to a heroic past, like the images of the despoiled land, reinforces the tragic irony of this poem. Drayton forecasts a bleak future for England and no future for the kind of poetry he had spent his life trying to write.

Divine Poems   Drayton concludes the 1630 folio collection with three divine poems, including *Moses His Birth and Miracles,* which had been published in 1604 as *Moses in a Map of his Miracles.* The subject matter of the two new divine poems, *Noahs Floud* and *David and Goliah,* appealed to Drayton because of his uncanny and accurate sense of impending disaster. He had watched men sow the divisive seeds that would mature as the English Civil War. The divine poems merit little literary attention, but they yield insights about Drayton's views at the end of his career. He selects the story of Noah's flood because it dramatizes God's destruction of the wicked. Noah's sermon to the impious threatens "Gods Vengeance upon the world" (162–225), echoing the railing passages in Drayton's *Elegies. David and Goliah,* artistically the most appealing of his divine poems, furnished Drayton with a congenial biblical hero. He describes David's physical charms with the erotic flair of his early complaints. David's musical talent enables him to charm the beasts and soothe the mad king Saul. His artistic talent turns David into an Orphic figure for Drayton. David also courageously accepts the challenge to act as Israel's champion against Goliah, thus figuring as the heroic man of arms, for whom Drayton exhibited lifelong respect. David, the heroic bard and soldier, harangues the Israelites:

> Despised nation, *Israel* quoth he,
> Where be those valiant men that liv'd in thee,
> What are our soules in lesser moulds now cast.
> (475–77)

The divine poems, like all of Drayton's late works, mourn the disappearance of heroic values in life and art.

Chapter Eight
Drayton's Legacy

Significance as Literary Critic

Drayton demonstrated his interest in literary history and criticism in his comments on genre in the 1619 folio and in his discussion of public as opposed to private poetry in *Poly-Olbion*. In his 1627 elegy addressed to "My Most Dearely-Loved Friend, Henery Reynolds Esquire, of Poets and Poesie," he offers an evaluation of English and Scottish poets beginning with Chaucer in the fourteenth century and concluding with William Browne in the seventeenth.[1] From a literary perspective, this elegy anticipates the verse epistles of literary criticism that became popular in the eighteenth century; his elegy may even have influenced Pope's *Essay on Criticism*.[2] Drayton's catalog defines a canon of English Renaissance poetry that deserves attention because it reveals the critical judgments of a practicing Renaissance poet. In this elegy he also expands on his important insights concerning the distinction between public and private poetry.

John Donne and Coterie Poetry   The most significant omission from Drayton's catalog is John Donne. Donne's *Anniversaries* appeared in print during Drayton's lifetime, but the bulk of his work was not published until after 1631, the year in which both Drayton and Donne died. Drayton's omission of Donne was deliberate. He explicitly states that he will concern himself only with those "[w]hose workes oft printed . . . To publique censure subject have bin most" (184–85). His reference to cabinet poems as "wonderous reliques" may be an allusion aimed at Donne's "The Relique."

> For such whose poems, be they nere so rare,
> In private chambers, that incloistered are,
> And by transcription daintyly must goe;
> As though the world unworthy were to know,
> Their rich composures, let those men that keepe
> These wonderous reliques in their judgement deepe, . . .
>   (187–92)

Drayton consigns the preservation of the "rich composures" and "wonderous reliques" of the chamber poets to those who will come after him. Although his antiquarian interests and literary activity insured his social acceptance by men who shared his interests, he was not by birth a member of the social milieu to which the coterie poets belonged.[3] He resented the elitist social assumptions of chamber poets who assumed that the world was "unworthy" to know their "wonderous reliques." Coterie poetry also lacked the heroic aspiration that Drayton required of poetry; the "closet" or "chamber" epic, as he realized, is a contradiction in terms.

Public Theater   Drayton began his career with a prejudice against the stage. In the eighth eclogue of *Idea The Shepheards Garland* he attacks contemporary dramatists who "strut the stage with reperfumed wordes" (4) and "rave it out in rime" (5). When Drayton revised this eclogue and published it as the fourth eclogue in the 1606 pastorals, he omitted these lines, replacing them with a more positive allusion to contemporary dramatists: "And in this season when the stirring Swaine / Makes the wide fields sound with thundring words" (3–4). His experience while working as a playwright in the summer of 1598 and periodically thereafter changed his views on the public theater.

Ben Jonson and William Shakespeare   Of the playwrights included in Drayton's catalog, Marlowe, Shakespeare, Jonson, Nashe, and Chapman, only Shakespeare and Jonson are praised for their work as playwrights. Drayton's critical appraisal of the relative talents of Shakespeare and Jonson emphasizes Shakespeare's natural talent in contrast to Jonson's learned art. His contrast was to become a commonplace for later criticism, establishing the principal grounds of comparison between Shakespeare and Jonson, later elaborated by John Dryden in the *Essay of Dramatic Poesy*. Shakespeare is described by Drayton as having a "naturall braine," "strong conception," and as "Cleere a rage, / As any one that trafiqu'd with the stage" (20–22). For Jonson, Drayton uses the epithet "learn'd":

> Who had drunke deepe of the *Pierian* spring,
> Whose knowledge did him worthily prefer,
> And long was Lord here of the Theater.
>   (129–32)

Drayton approves of Jonson's insistence upon the unities of action, time, and place by referring to "Poems rightly dramatique" (139).

William Drummond of Hawthornden's account of enmity between Drayton and Jonson ought to be approached skeptically. Drummond had begun a correspondence with Drayton in 1618, and he probably tried to get Jonson to discuss Drayton, whom he had not met. In the *Conversations with Drummond* Jonson mentions that Drayton was attacked for using the possessive case in the title of his *Mortimeriados* (1596) and that Sir John Davies had "played in ane Epigrame on Drayton."[4] It is unlikely that in 1619 Jonson would recall an epigram written more than twenty-five years earlier unless Drummond had "primed the pump." By 1627 Drayton and Jonson regarded each other as comrades, survivors of a passing generation. Both had lived during the reign of Elizabeth, but there were younger writers growing up who had only experienced the Stuart courts.

His Canon of Poets   Drayton's canon of poets is unconventional because he includes a prose pamphleteer, translators, and Scottish poets in his catalog. The high value that he put on satire as a genre is suggested by his including among the poets Thomas Nashe, who wrote most of his work in prose. In so doing, Drayton follows Sidney who regarded "feigning," or the creation of a fiction, as more essential to poetry than meter or rhyme. He also praises Sidney for eradicating the influence of John Lyly's *Euphues* on English prose and devotes a full eight lines to Nashe's satirical prose. In addition to treating prose fiction as poetry, Drayton comments on translators as poets, even though their works lack originality. Of the many translators of his age, he singles out George Chapman and George Sandys for unqualified praise, but expresses reservations about Joshua Sylvester's "owne invention." Finally, Drayton's warm praise of Scottish writers, Sir William Alexander and William Drummond of Hawthornden, suggests that he was one of the first to regard Scottish poetry as part of a British tradition.

Contemporaries' Criticism

Little applied criticism of the work of sixteenth- and seventeenth-century poets has survived, but by examining specific images and tag phrases consistently used to describe a particular poet, it is possible to learn what poetic characteristics impressed his contemporaries. Bernard Weinberg labeled this phenomenon, "criticism by epithet."[5] Eventually, tag phrases were replaced by critical evaluations deriving from systematic theory, but epithets and descriptive phrases, when repeated with sufficient consistency, serve as a rudimentary guide to applied criticism during the late sixteenth and early seventeenth centuries. Using this method of inquiry to assess Drayton's po-

etic values, Joan Grundy has suggested that his use of "clear" as a complimentary epithet signals his appreciation of visionary poetry and of Marlowe's
heroic figures.[6]

Drayton's contemporaries praised his learning and called him "golden-
mouthed." The third eclogue of Thomas Lodge's satire, *A Fig for Momus,* is
dedicated to Drayton as Rowland. In this dialogue between Wagrin and
Golde, Wagrin tried to persuade Golde that to serve the arts and learning is
worthwhile; Golde, however, persists in wanting a reward: "I rest resolu'd, if
bountie will, I wright, / If not, why then my muse shall flie the light"
(9,596).[7] Lodge's epistle 5, also addressed to Michael Drayton, explains that
the low reputation of poets is caused by those who "by scurrility / Would
purchase fame and immortality" (9–10). Contending that true excellence in
poetry requires that the verse be "aim'd to good and happy ends," Lodge
praises Drayton's "learned nines and threes" (49), alluding to the Neoplatonic lore that Drayton inserted in *Ideas Mirrour* (1594) and *Endimion
and Phoebe* (1595).

Drayton's imitation of classical genres in *Englands Heroicall Epistles* and
Poly-Olbion, as well as his research in the antiquarian chronicles, established
him as poet with a claim to learning. The poet John Weever emphasizes his
learning and wit in his twenty-third epigram, a poem addressed to Drayton
in *Epigrammes in the Oldest Cut and Newest Fashion* (1599):

> The Peeres of heav'n kept a parliament,
> And for Wittes-mirrour *Philip Sidney* sent,
> To keepe another when they doe intend,
> Twentie to one for *Drayton* they will send,
>   Yet bade him leave his learning, so it fled,
>   And vow'd to live with thee since he was dead.[8]

To be favorably compared with Sidney, the poet and courtier, whose reputation for learning had spread throughout Europe, was indeed high praise.

The epithet "golden mouth" was also applied to Drayton with some consistency as a tribute to his oratorical qualities. In satire 6 of *Skialetheia*
Everard Guilpin summarizes contemporary criticism of Drayton and offers
a defense:

> *Drayton's* condemn'd of some for imitation,
> But others say t'was the best Poets fashion,
> In spight of sicke Opinions crooked doome,
> Traytor to kingdome mind, true iudgments toomb,

> Like to a worthy *Romaine* he hath wonne
> A three-fold name affined to the *Sunne,*
> When he is mounted in the glorious South,
> And *Drayton's* justly sirnam'd *Golden-mouth.*
>
> (85–92)[9]

By juxtaposing "sicke Opinions crooked doome" with "kingdome mind," the tomb or last resting place of true judgment, Guilpin suggests that those who are properly informed will understand that Drayton's art involves the appropriate use of models for imitation. He also alludes approvingly to the use of the epithet "golden-mouthed" for Drayton in Charles Fitzgeoffrey's *Sir Francis Drake* (1596). Historically, the phrase "golden-mouthed" was used to render the surname, Chrysostom, of Dio and of John Chrysostom, both of whom were famous for their oratorical talent. Francis Meres in *Palladis Tamia* (1598) comments that Drayton is described as " 'golden-mouthed' for the purity and preciousness of his style and phrase."[10] For Drayton's contemporaries, the term "golden-mouthed" carried with it the suggestion of clever and copious rhetoric. But Drayton's rhetorical flourishes and learned conceits earned him ridicule as well as admiration. Most of the satire directed at Drayton accuses him of introducing incongruously learned allusions into love poetry.

Reputation

Restoration and Eighteenth Century   In the only study focusing specifically on Drayton's literary reputation, Russell Noyes in 1935 mistakenly described his stature as waning at the time of his death and sinking almost into oblivion during the years of Dryden and Pope: "Dryden's birth date (1631) is the year of Drayton's death, and Pope's death (1744) comes just four years before the mid-century revival of Drayton ushered in by a folio edition of his works. The expanse of years, then, covered by the lives of these two dominant classicists very neatly marks Drayton's 'period of obscurity.'"[11] That Drayton was buried in Westminster Abbey near Edmund Spenser indicates that his reputation was at a high point when he died. Both Sir Thomas Browne and Robert Burton made use of Drayton's work.[12] The antiquary William Fulman (1632–88) describes Drayton's funeral as an impressive ceremony; he says that "the Gentlemen of the Four Innes of Court and others of note about the Town, [reached] in order by two and two, from his Lodging [in Fleet Street] almost to Strandbridge" (Newdigate, 219). His association with Selden, who wrote the notes for *Poly-Olbion,* and the high esteem he had achieved by the time he died led the next generation to place him in the company of Chaucer, Spenser, and Shakespeare.

In 1675 Edward Phillips, Milton's nephew, ranks Drayton with Edmund Spenser and Sir Philip Sidney: "*Michael Drayton,* contemporary of *Spenser* and *Sir Philip Sydney,* and for fame and renown in poetry, not much inferior in his time to either."[13] The assessment that Phillips offers in *Theatrum Poetarum* affords a summary of the critical attitudes toward Drayton that prevailed in the new generation: "however he seems somewhat antiquated in the esteem of the more curious of these times, especially in his *Polyalbion.* . . . His *England's Heroical Epistles* are more generally liked; and to such as love the pretty chat of Nymphs and Shepherds his *Nymphals* and other things of that nature cannot be unpleasant." Although Phillips mentions Drayton's "*Nymphals* and other things of that nature," referring to *The Muses Elizium, Nimphidia, The Quest of Cynthia,* and *The Shepheards Sirena,* he ignores Drayton's historical poetry entirely except for *Englands Heroicall Epistles.* His early pastorals and sonnets are not mentioned, nor are his satires, elegies, and odes.

In 1637 a posthumous collected edition of his works appeared; the next complete edition of Drayton was not printed until over a century later in 1748. Because Noyes relied on editions as the only standard for judging Drayton's literary reputation, he wrongly concluded that Drayton became obscure during the Restoration and eighteenth century.

Englands Heroicall Epistles remained popular during the eighteenth century, stimulating a long list of modernizations, imitations, and even reprints without acknowledgment. In his study of the influence of the Elizabethans on the eighteenth century, Earl R. Wasserman identifies *Englands Heroicall Epistles* as second only to *The Faerie Queene* in its popularity and influence.[14] That *Englands Heroicall Epistles* appealed to the Augustans is not surprising. The classical authority of Ovid's *Heroides* helped to legitimize Drayton's exchange of letters between lovers in English history. The orthodoxy of the genre was further confirmed when Alexander Pope published his own heroic epistle, *Eloisa to Abelard,* in 1717.[15] Metrics too played a role: *Englands Heroicall Epistles* was written in heroic couplets, a verse form congenial to the Augustans. Nearer the end of the century Samuel Johnson returned again and again to Drayton's work for quotations in his *Dictionary.*[16]

Nineteenth Century   To determine the degree of Drayton's continued popularity in the nineteenth century, it would be necessary to examine verse anthologies and small press publications.[17] The list of British writers who echo Drayton or reveal even more substantial kinds of influence includes

Blake,[18] Wordsworth,[19] Coleridge,[20] Keats,[21] and Tennyson.[22] In the United States his influence on poets has not been well documented, but Edwin Whipple, the influential critic who did much to establish Hawthorne's reputation, comments on Drayton as well as Spenser and Daniel.[23]

Assessment

Assessment of Drayton poses extraordinary difficulties. He is one of the few English Renaissance poets who revised his works after they were in print, and in some cases he did so repeatedly. Even though Drayton intended his 1619 revisions of his Elizabethan works to serve as authoritative texts, there are critics who prefer *Mortimeriados* (1596) to *The Barons Warres* (1603, 1619) because qualities are lost as well as gained through his extensive revisions. It is also difficult to classify the kind of poet Drayton was. He wrote in so many genres that his stature as a poet will fluctuate with shifts in critical taste and with scholarly trends. His *Englands Heroicall Epistles, Legends,* and *The Baron Warres* may receive more attention from the "new historicists" than they did from the "new critics." His lengthy historical works do not lend themselves to the close reading that has been in vogue for the past generation.

It should also be acknowledged that what a previous generation valued in Drayton has made him unfashionable to the present. Labels, such as conservative and patriotic, have not weathered well. Since Drayton was one of the two or three most "anti-establishment" poets of his age, those labels need reassessment. The scholarly lenses through which we have viewed his works have made him seem less interesting as a literary figure than in fact he was. If "conservative" means writing "safe" poems in approved genres, then Drayton was far from conservative. He continued to write about the reign of Edward II and Edward's male "minions" after James came to the throne and began to promote a series of male favorites. His generic experiments are legion—the chorographical poem, the ode, the nymphal in the late pastorals. Finally, if in the seventeenth century "patriotic" meant tacit loyalty to a king who was believed to rule by divine appointment, then Drayton was far from a patriot. In his late works kings persistently appear as tyrants who threaten traditional liberties. If, as Richard Helgerson has recently argued, love of country gradually displaced allegiance to the sovereign in early modern England, we need to rethink the terminology we use in discussing Drayton's politics.[24]

In addition to the problems of assessment particular to Drayton, we encounter difficulties intrinsic to evaluation. Of the many kinds of indices of reputation, to which do we give most weight? Drayton's *Englands Heroicall Epistles* achieved popular and critical success in its own day. These poems continued to be a critical success, to be imitated and adapted during the Restoration and eighteenth century, but his fairy poems, *Nimphidia* particularly, were successful in a popular market in the eighteenth and nineteenth centuries. That market probably would not have paid attention either to Ovid's *Heroides* or to *Englands Heroicall Epistles*.

Using accessibility, the availability of modern editions, as a measure of stature and appreciation, Russell Noyes claimed that Drayton was all but forgotten after his death until he was "rediscovered" in the nineteenth century. In this regard, it should be noted that the number of editions a poet receives has to be interpreted very carefully. English literature was not an academic subject in universities until late in the nineteenth century; university-educated men read the classics. Both Byron and Shelley were influenced by Greek and Latin literature. Keats, one of the few romantic poets who read widely in English literature, owned a copy of Drayton's work and echoes him in a number of poems.[25] The increased number of editions of Drayton as we move into the twentieth century can also be deceiving. A. H. Bullen's selective edition of Drayton's work was printed in 125 copies.

The historical period courses that constitute the framework of the academic curriculum encourage classification. Although Drayton was born almost a decade before Jonson and Donne, his work, until recently, has been approached as an Elizabethan survival rather than as a Jacobean critique.[26] Much of Drayton's work has been left unread or ignored. In spite of his own conviction that he had surpassed Samuel Daniel in the historical epic, Daniel's work has prompted a number of articles while Drayton's histories have generated only two articles written by Kathleen Tillotson, one of his editors. Studies of his entire body of work have glanced at *The Owle, The Moon-calfe,* and *The Elegies,* but these poems have never received critical attention as individual works. In the seventeenth century Abraham Holland identified Drayton's classical masters as Ovid, Lucan, and Juvenal (Newdigate, 199). The Juvenalian satire in Drayton's late works has been virtually ignored.

Drayton was an heir to the great humanist tradition that elevated epic poetry above other genres. *The Barons Warres, Poly-Olbion,* and *The Battaile of Agincourt* were intended as epics. His view of the poet as a public spokesman for the national consciousness puts Drayton in an English tradition that derives from Spenser and anticipates Milton. Less politically astute than Spenser and born a decade later, Drayton never won the favor of the powerful elite who governed England. While Jonson, Daniel, Campion, and Fletcher were recognized as poets and invited to supply masques and entertainments for the royal family, Drayton was ignored.

Because he was isolated from literary patronage focused in the court, he was more sensitive to the movement away from public poetry that occurred during his lifetime. The entire body of Drayton's work affords fascinating insight into the mind of a critically aware poet who understood that the role of the poet was changing. *The Muses Elizium,* previously treated as a celebration of the golden world of poetic imagination, has been reinterpreted above in the context of his last work. After completing the second part of *Poly-Olbion,* Drayton believed that epic poetry, and the values it embodied, could no longer be written with conviction. He left *Poly-Olbion* unfinished just as Colin Clout breaks his pipe before *The Faerie Queene* is complete. In *The Muses Elizium* Poly-Olbion, the "very happy land," ironically becomes "Felicia," a society without respect for its history and without interest in humane letters. In his last imaginative work, Drayton forecasts that poetry will turn to satire and romantic escape, to jeremiad and idyll. He was only partly wrong. A great epic poem was written in the generation after his death, but Milton's epic was not an Arthurian English epic celebrating Albion.

In the last lines of *The Muses Elizium* Drayton dismisses Felicia as a land peopled by "fooles and madmen" (141). Almost prophesying the Civil War, he forecasts "plagues that shortly are to come" (121). At the end of his career, Drayton abandoned his nostalgia for the past "glorious age" of England. His last poem concludes with bitterness against "the cruell kinde" who turned him from an aspiring laureate to a lonely Satyr.

Appendix A: Goodere of Polesworth Genealogy

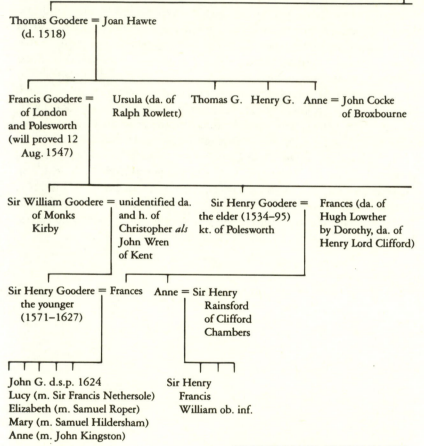

John Goodere = (will proved 14 Feb. 1513–14)

Thomas Goodere = Joan Hawte (d. 1518)

Francis Goodere = of London and Polesworth (will proved 12 Aug. 1547) — Ursula (da. of Ralph Rowlett) — Thomas G. — Henry G. — Anne = John Cocke of Broxbourne

Sir William Goodere of Monks Kirby = unidentified da. and h. of Christopher *als* John Wren of Kent — Sir Henry Goodere = the elder (1534–95) kt. of Polesworth — Frances (da. of Hugh Lowther by Dorothy, da. of Henry Lord Clifford)

Sir Henry Goodere = Frances the younger (1571–1627) — Anne = Sir Henry Rainsford of Clifford Chambers

John G. d.s.p. 1624
Lucy (m. Sir Francis Nethersole)
Elizabeth (m. Samuel Roper)
Mary (m. Samuel Hildersham)
Anne (m. John Kingston)

Sir Henry
Francis
William ob. inf.

FITZWILLIAMS-COOKE-BACON-

Ursula Rowlett's mother, Sir Henry Goodere's grandmother, was Margaret, daughter of Sir Anthony Cooke of Gidea Hall, Essex, by Anne, daughter of Sir William Fitzwilliams. Sir Anthony Cooke's daughter, Mildred, was married to Sir William Cecil, Lord Burghley, and his daughter Anne to Sir Nicholas Bacon. Sir Henry therefore was first cousin once removed to Sir Robert Cecil, Earl of Salisbury, and also to Anthony and Francis Bacon. He was great-nephew to William Cooke of St. Martin's-in-the-Fields and first cousin once removed

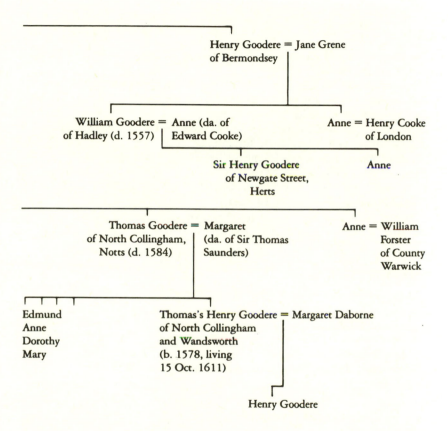

CECIL-ROWLETT-GOODERE-SIDNEY

to the younger Sir Anthony Cooke. Sir William Fitzwilliams's grandson, Sir William (d. 1599), married Anne, daughter of Sir William Sidney and aunt to Sir Philip Sidney.

Key: d. = died, da. = daughter, m. = married, b. = born, kt. = knight, ob. inf. = died as infant, d.s.b. = died without issue, h. = heir, *als* = also. Adapted from Bernard H. Newdigate, *Michael Drayton and His Circle* (1941; reprint; Oxford: Basil Blackwell & Mott, 1961), 227.

Appendix B: Drayton's Plays

1598

The Famous Wars of Henry I and the Prince of Wales (with Henry Chettle, Thomas Dekker)
Earl Goodwin and his Three Sons, part 1 (with Chettle, Dekker, Robert Wilson)
Earl Goodwin and his Three Sons, part 2 (with Chettle, Dekker, Wilson)
Pierce of Exton (with Chettle, Dekker, Wilson)
The Funeral of Richard Coeur-de-Lion (with Chettle, Anthony Munday, Wilson)
Chance Medley (with Chettle or Dekker, Munday, Wilson)
The Civil Wars of France, part 1 (with Dekker)
The Civil Wars of France, part 2 (with Dekker)
The Civil Wars of France, part 3 (with Dekker)
Connan Prince of Cornwall (with Dekker)
Hannibal and Hermes, or Worse afeared than Hurt, part 1 (with Dekker)
Hannibal and Hermes, part 2 (with Dekker)
The Madman's Morris (with Dekker, Wilson)
Pierce of Winchester (with Dekker, Wilson)
Mother Redcap (with Munday)

1599

William Longsword
Sir John Oldcastle, part 1 (with Richard Hathway, Munday, Wilson)

June 1600–January 1601

Fair Constance of Rome, part 1 (with Dekker, Hathway, Munday, Wilson)
Fair Constance of Rome, part 2 (with Hathway and others)
Sir John Oldcastle, part 2 (with Hathway, Munday, Wilson)
Owen Tudor (with Hathway, Munday, Wilson)

August 1601

The Life and Rising of Cardinal Wolsey (with Chettle, Munday, Wentworth Smith)

July–August 1602

Caesar's Fall, or the Two Shapes (with Dekker, Thomas Middleton, Munday, John Webster)

January 1604 (?1603–1605)

The London Prodigal (possibly a collaborator)

Notes and References

Preface

1. Edward Phillips, *Theatrum Poetarum Anglicanorum: Containing the Names and Characters of All the English Poets from the Reign of Henry III to the Close of the Reign of Queen Elizabeth,* revised by Samuel Egerton Brydges (Canterbury: J. White, 1800), 262–71.
2. Mario Praz, "Michael Drayton," *English Studies* 28 (1947):97–107.
3. *The Works of Michael Drayton,* ed. J. William Hebel, Kathleen Tillotson, and Bernard H. Newdigate, 5 vols. (1941; Oxford: Basil Blackwell for the Shakespeare Head Press, 1961), 5:xiv.

Chapter One

1. Richard F. Hardin, *Michael Drayton and the Passing of Elizabethan England* (Lawrence: University of Kansas, 1973), 9–10.
2. *The Works of Michael Drayton,* ed. Charles Coffey (London: R. Dodsley, J. Jolliffe, and W. Reeve, 1748), 3. This life of Drayton was written under the supervision of William Oldys, who concludes that since no incident of Drayton's life was recorded "by any other Pen than his own, we have to derive his biography from his works." (3); hereafter cited in the text as "Oldys," followed by page number.
3. Bernard H. Newdigate, *Michael Drayton and His Circle* (1941; Oxford: Basil Blackwell & Mott, 1961); hereafter cited in the text as "Newdigate," followed by page number.
4. For background, see *Patronage in the Renaissance,* ed. Guy Fitch Lytle and Stephen Orgel (Princeton: Princeton University Press, 1981), esp. Linda Levy Peck, "Court Patronage and Government Policy: The Jacobean Dilemma," 27–46.
5. All references are to *The Works of Michael Drayton,* ed. Hebel, Tillotson, and Newdigate. First references to verse are cited parenthetically by volume, page, and line numbers (e.g., 3:226.22–23); references to prefaces and prose are cited by volume and page numbers (e.g., 3:226); following references are cited by line or page numbers as appropriate.

Although Drayton repeatedly and extensively revised his poetry for every pre-1619 publication, his editors have used the 1619 folio versions as the copy text for the modern standard edition. The pre-1619 versions of prefaces, dedications, and passages are printed as textual variants in volume 5 of the standard edition (cited throughout as "Tillotson" because it also contains the notes prepared by Kathleen Tillotson). Since I am examining Drayton's work chronologically, parenthetical references to Tillotson are important and frequent.

6. Oldys's biography remained standard until *Poems by Michael Drayton,* ed. J. Payne Collier, Roxburghe Club (London: J. B. Nichols, 1856). Collier was the first scholar to check the Mancetter parish records, but he found that the existing books went back no further than 1576 (iv); hereafter cited in the text as "Collier," followed by page number.

7. Oliver Elton, *Michael Drayton: A Critical Study* (London: Archibald Constable & Co., 1905), 5.

8. The court case is cataloged in the Public Record Office as Goodier v. Goodier; PRO 4 Jas. Chancery: Town Depositions, Bundle 313. For a transcript of Drayton's testimony, see Kathleen Tillotson, "Drayton and the Gooderes," *Modern Language Review* 35 (1940):341–49.

9. Jean Robertson, "Drayton and the Countess of Pembroke," *Review of English Studies* 16, n.s. (1965):49.

10. On 26 February 1620 Sir Dudley Carleton wrote, "I forgat in my last that Sir Fra: Nethersole was then newly married to Mistris Goodyeare that served the Lady of Bedford who gave her 500li or 700li, besides 500li she bestowed upon them in gloves, which brought in a great contribution of plate to make up a portion which her father Sir Henry could not geve" (*The Letters of John Chamberlain,* ed. Norman E. McClure [Philadelphia: American Philosophical Society, 1939], 2:291).

11. Frank Whigham, *Ambition and Privilege: The Social Tropes of Elizabethan Courtesy Theory* (Berkeley: University of California Press, 1984).

12. For Jonson's skill in manipulating the patronage system, see Stanley Fish, "Authors-Readers: Jonson's Community of the Same," in *Representing the English Renaissance,* ed. Stephen Greenblatt (Berkeley: University of California Press, 1988), 231–64.

13. Alfred Harbage, *Annals of English Drama (975–1700),* revised by Samuel Schoenbaum (Philadelphia: University of Pennsylvania Press, 1964), 66–67, 70–71, 76–79, 82–83; E. K. Chambers, *The Elizabethan Stage* (Oxford: Clarendon Press, 1923), 3:306–8.

14. See also Richard Hardin's bibliography on Drayton as a playwright in *The Popular School,* ed. T. P. Logan and D. S. Smith (Lincoln: University of Nebraska Press, 1975), 137–45.

15. For a genealogical survey, see Christopher Whitfield, "Clifford Chambers: The Muses Quiet Port," *Notes and Queries,* October 1965, 362–75.

16. For evidence that the Astons collected and wrote poetry, see *Tixall Poetry,* ed. Arthur Clifford (Edinburgh: James Ballantyne & Co., 1813).

17. Hardin, *Michael Drayton,* 77; cf. Joan Grundy, *The Spenserian Poets: A Study in Elizabethan and Jacobean Poetry* (London: Edward Arnold, 1969), 10.

18. *A Transcript of the Registers of the Company of Stationers, 1554–1640,* 5 vols., ed. Edward Arber (London, 1875–94), 2:836.

19. Henry Chettle, *Englandes Mourning Garment: Worne here by plaine Shepheardes; in memorie of their sacred Mistresse, Elizabeth, queene of Vertue . . . To which is added the true manner of her Emperiall Funerall* (1603) in *Shakespeare*

Allusion-Books, ed. C. M. Ingleby, New Shakespeare Society, ser. 4, no. 1 (London: N. Truebner, 1874), 72–74.

20. See J[ohn] F[enton], *King James His Welcome To London With Elizaes Tombe and Epitaph* (London: Thomas Pavier, 1603), sig. C4.

> . . . another all to torne,
> Greets the 'n a garment thats by shepheards worne.
> A proper worke of learned Poetry?
> Of Oratory: Proase? and Heraldry?
> A rare conceited piece of worke no doubt?
> Whose sharpe conceite younger conceites doth flout.
> Well he is learned, and were I but able,
> He should eate bread from our *Augustus* stable.

Fenton dismisses Chettle as fit only to eat bread from James's stable because his attacks on Daniel, Shakespeare, Drayton, and others were so self-serving. Likewise in epigram 12 in *Epigrammes* (1604?) by I. C. Gent, Chettle's slanderous attack on his contemporaries is deplored as a calculated attempt to "whet the buyer on" (see *Shakespeare Allusion Books,* ed. C. M. Ingleby, 121–22).

21. For Lucy's patronage of Daniel, Jonson, and Donne, see Barbara Lewalski's "Lucy, Countess of Bedford: Images of a Jacobean Courtier and Patroness," in *Politics of Discourse: The Literature and History of Seventeenth Century England,* ed. Kevin Sharpe and Steven Zwicker (Berkeley: University of California Press, 1987), 52–77.

22. *The Progresses, Processions, and Magnificent Festivities of King James the First,* 3 vols., ed. John Nichols (London: J. B. Nichols, 1828), 1:180.

23. For evidence that dedications were retained by the printers until 1619, see Dick Taylor, "Drayton and the Countess of Bedford," *Studies in Philology* 49 (1952):214–28.

24. M. J. Dickson, "William Trevell and the Whitefriars Theatre," *Review of English Studies* 6 (1930):309–12; and Margaret Dowling, "Further Notes on William Trevell," *Review of English Studies* 6 (1930):443–46.

25. Newdigate, 182. For other copies of their correspondence, see *The Works of William Drummond of Hawthornden* (Edinburgh: James Watson, 1711), 153–54; 233–34.

26. PRO, C 66/2197, no. 8. Cited in R. C. Bald, *John Donne, a Life* (Oxford: Oxford University Press, 1970), 494.

27. Henry Peacham, *The Truth of Our Times* (London, 1638), 38; cited in Newdigate, 221–22.

Chapter Two

1. For background on this work, see Stanley Stewart, *The Enclosed Garden: The Tradition and the Image in Seventeenth-Century Poetry* (Madison: University of Wisconsin Press, 1966), 4–5.

2. For a discussion of Spenser, Jonson, and Milton as "self-crowned laureates" and Drayton's laureate gestures, see Richard Helgerson, *Self-Crowned Laureates* (Berkeley and Los Angeles: University of California Press, 1983), 33–34, 255.

3. For the Vergilian framework, see Michael D. Bristol, "Structural Patterns in Two Elizabethan Pastorals," *Studies in English Literature* 10 (1970):33–48.

4. Unless otherwise noted, references throughout this chapter are to the texts of poems printed in volume 1 of the standard edition. Line numbers are cited parenthetically in the text, and page numbers are cited when the reference is to a preface or prose dedication.

5. Joan Grundy, "'Brave Translunary Things,'" *Modern Language Review* 59 (1964):501–10.

6. Kathleen Tillotson, "Spenser's 'Aetion,'" *Times Literary Supplement,* 7 February 1935, 76.

7. Lines 444–47. *Spenser's Minor Poems,* 3 vols., ed. Ernest de Selincourt (Oxford: Clarendon Press, 1910), 1:321.

8. Kathleen Tillotson, "The Language of Drayton's *Shepheards Garland,*" *Review of English Studies* 13 (1937):272–81.

9. On Elizabeth I as Astraea, see Frances A. Yates, *Astraea: The Imperial Theme in the Sixteenth Century* (London and Boston: Routledge & Kegan Paul, 1975).

10. In eclogue 8, *Poemes Lyrick and pastorall* (1606), Drayton bitterly satirizes false patronesses and alludes to Anne Goodere as Idea (2:109–26), but it distorts the record of Drayton's early clientage connections to use a 1606 allusion to gloss *Ideas Mirrour* (1594).

11. Lauro Martines, *Society and History in English Renaissance Verse* (Oxford: Basil Blackwell, 1985), 27.

12. "25. In Decium," *Works of Sir John Davies,* ed. Robert Krueger (Oxford: Clarendon Press, 1975), 139. See Ben Jonson's *Conversations with William Drummond of Hawthornden* in Ben Jonson, *The Complete Poems,* ed. George Parfitt (Baltimore: Penguin, 1975), 466 (lines 181–84). Hereafter cited as Jonson, *Poems,* ed. Parfitt.

13. VI.i.245–64 in *Collected Poems of Joseph Hall, Bishop of Exeter and Norwich,* ed. A. Davenport (Liverpool: University Press, 1949), lii, 94–95; and Sidney H. Atkins, "Who Was 'Labeo'?" *Times Literary Supplement,* 4 July 1936, 304.

14. For excellent analyses of this genre, see the introduction to *Elizabethan Minor Epics,* ed. Elizabeth Story Donno (New York: Columbia University Press, 1963), 1–20; and Clark Hulse, *Metamorphic Verse: The Elizabethan Minor Epic* (Princeton: Princeton University Press, 1981), 3–34.

15. John Buxton, in *A Tradition of Poetry* (New York: Macmillan, 1967), 71, states that "*Endimion and Phoebe* was written for the marriage in December 1594 of Lucy Harington (then not quite fourteen) to the young Earl of Bedford," but gives no particulars.

16. Grundy, in "'Brave Translunary Things,'" 505–7, first suggested that *Endimion and Phoebe* was an allegory of poetic inspiration. Barbara C. Ewell, in "Drayton's *Endimion and Phoebe:* An Allegory of Aesthetics," *Explorations in Renaissance Culture* 7 (1981):15–26, develops this suggestion into an allegorical reading in which "art, as verbally enfleshed Beauty, reveals to men the intellectual Beauty of the ideal" (24). For a more Neoplatonic reading, see Vincent F. Petronella, "Double Ecstasy in Drayton's *Endimion and Phoebe,*" *Studies in English Literature* 24 (1984): 87–104. Of the two visions, Petronella says: "The first involves the body's surrendering to the soul; the second deals with the soul's separation from the body in full mystical ecstasy" (98).

17. Ben Jonson, *The Forest,* epistle xii., a New Year's gift to Elizabeth, Countess of Rutland: "You, and that other starre, that purest light, / Of all *Lucina*'s traine; *Lucy* the bright" (65–66). Jonson, *Poems,* ed. Parfitt, 112.

18. For the political focus of *Mirror for Magistrates,* see Lily B. Campbell, ed., *The Mirror for Magistrates* (Cambridge: Cambridge University Press, 1938), 3–60, esp. 111.

19. Hulse, *Metamorphic Verse,* 24–26.

20. Scott Giantvalley, in "Barnfield, Drayton, and Marlowe: Homoeroticism and Homosexuality in Elizabethan Literature," *Pacific Coast Philology* 16 (1981):9–24, suggests the difficulty in assessing Elizabethan attitudes toward homosexual love. Since Drayton never married, late nineteenth-century insistence upon his life-long devotion to Anne Goodere may have been prompted by concern about his sexual preferences.

21. Francis Meres, *Palladis Tamia,* ed. Don Cameron Allen, University of Illinois Studies in Language and Literature, 16 (Urbana: University of Illinois Press, 1933), 75; hereafter cited parenthetically in the text. For Elizabethan thoughts on epic, see Lewis F. Ball, "The Background of the Minor English Renaissance Epics," *English Literary History* (1934):63–89.

22. Hardin, *Michael Drayton,* 33–34.

Chapter Three

1. *Englands Heroicall Epistles* is printed in volume 2 of the standard edition; the 1619 edition was used as the copy text for all poems in this volume. The following discussion focuses on dedications and passages, appearing in 1597, 1598, 1599, and 1600 editions of *Englands Heroicall Epistles,* material deleted from the 1619 edition and printed in volume 5 (cited as Tillotson). First references to prefaces and dedications remaining in the 1619 text are cited parenthetically as (volume 2:page

number) and as (volume 2.line number) for verse references; later references will be to either page or line number as appropriate.

2. For comparative discussion of Ovid and Drayton, see N. Christoph de Nagy, *Michael Drayton's "Englands Heroicall Epistles": A Study in Themes and Compositional Devices,* Cooper Monographs, 14 (Bern: Francke, 1968).

3. On the *Heroides,* see Florence Verducci, *Ovid's Toyshop of the Heart, "Epistulae Heroidum"* (Princeton: Princeton University Press, 1985), esp. 4–32.

4. Attribution of these six to Ovid has been questioned but is now generally accepted. See Edward Kennard Rand, *Ovid and His Influence* (New York: Cooper Square Publishers, 1963), 17–33.

5. Katherine D. Carter, "Drayton's Craftsmanship: The Encomium and the Blazon in *Englands Heroicall Epistles,*" *Huntington Library Quarterly* 38 (1975):297–314.

6. George Puttenham, *The Arte of English Poesie* (1589), chapter 19, in *Elizabethan Critical Essays,* 2 vols., ed. G. Gregory Smith (Oxford: Clarendon Press, 1904), 2:41.

7. Ibid. See also Sir Thomas Elyot, *The Booke named The Governour,* ed. S. E. Lehmberg, Everyman's Library (1962; London: Dent, 1975), 36.

8. Cf. Barbara C. Ewell, "Unity and the Transformation of Drayton's Poetics in *Englands Heroicall Epistles,*" *Modern Language Quarterly* 44 (1983):231–50, and "From Idea to Act: The New Aesthetics of Drayton's *Englands Heroicall Epistles,*" *Journal of English and Germanic Philology* 82 (1983):515–25.

9. Hardin, *Michael Drayton,* 45–54, esp. 48.

10. Richard F. Hardin, "Convention and Design in Drayton's *Heroicall Epistles,*" *Publications of the Modern Language Association* 83 (1968):5–41.

11. *Stationers' Register,* ed. Arber, 3:677–78. For a suggestive study of topical references and censorship, see Annabel Patterson, *Censorship and Interpretation: The Conditions of Writing and Reading in Early Modern England* (Madison: University of Wisconsin Press, 1985), 44–119.

12. "These trifles may lead to mischief of serious consequence, if once made an object of ridicule and used in a serious manner."

13. For valuable background, see David Norbrook, *Poetry and Politics in the English Renaissance* (London: Routledge & Kegan Paul, 1984), 175.

14. See J. E. Neale, *Elizabeth I and her Parliaments, 1584–1601,* 2 vols. (London: Jonathon Cape, 1953–57), 2:251–66. See also Joel Hurstfield, "The Succession Struggle in Late Elizabethan England," *Elizabethan Government and Society: Essays Presented to Sir John Neale,* ed. S. T. Bindoff, J. Hurstfield, C. H. Williams (London: University of London Press, 1961), 369–96, esp. 384–86.

15. R. Doleman [Father Robert Parsons], *A Conference about the Next Succession to the crowne of England* (London: n.p., 1594), part 1, F4v; hereafter signatures are cited parenthetically in the text.

16. Parsons, *A Declaration of the True Causes of the Great Troubles, Presupposed to be Intended against the Realme of England* (London, 1592), E2v. In the same

passage Parsons refers to Spenser's *Mother Hubberds Tale* as the tale "of the false fox and his crooked cubbes," allusions to the Cecils.

17. For the cult of honor and military achievement associated with Essex, see Mervyn James, *Society, Politics and Culture: Studies in Early Modern England* (Cambridge: Cambridge University Press, 1986), 416–65, esp. 426.

18. *Calendar of State Papers, Domestic Series, 1595–1597,* ed. Mary Anne Everett Green (London: Longmans, Green, & Co., 1869), 158.

19. Lily B. Campbell, "The use of Historical Patterns in the Reign of Elizabeth," *Huntington Library Quarterly* 1 (1938):135–67. I am indebted to Campbell for a number of references discussed in this chapter.

20. William Camden, *The Historie of the Most Renowned and Victorious Princesse Elizabeth* (London: Benjamin Fisher, 1630), Booke 4, Hhhlv (57).

21. Arthur Collins, *Letters and Memorials of State* (London: T. Osborne, 1746), 1:350.

22. For a brief but valuable statement on the "new historicist" interpretation of *Richard II,* see Stephen Greenblatt's introduction to *The Power of Forms in the English Renaissance,* ed. Greenblatt (Norman: University of Oklahoma Press, 1982), 3–6. See also Evelyn May Albright, "Shakespeare's *Richard II* and the Essex Conspiracy." *PMLA* 42 (1927):686–720; Raymond Heffner, "Shakespeare, Hayward, and Essex," *PMLA* 45 (1930):754–80; Albright, "Shakespeare's *Richard II,* Hayward's History of Henry IV, and the Essex Conspiracy," *PMLA* 46 (1931):694–719.

23. Everard Guilpin, *Skialetheia,* ed. D. Allen Carroll (Chapel Hill: University of North Carolina Press, 1974), 65; hereafter cited parenthetically in the text.

24. *Calendar of State Papers, Domestic Series, 1598–1601,* ed. Mary Anne Everett Green (London: Longmans, Green & Co., 1869), 449; hereafter cited as *CSP, Dom, 1598–1601.*

25. Carole Levin, "Lady Jane Grey: Protestant Queen and Martyr," in *Silent But for the Word: Tudor Women as Patrons, Translators, and Writers of Religion,* ed. Margaret Patterson Hannay (Kent, Ohio: Kent State University Press, 1985), 92–106.

26. Laura Hanes Cadwallader, *The Career of the Earl of Essex from the Islands Voyage in 1597 to his Execution in 1601* (Philadelphia: University of Pennsylvania, 1923), 27–28. See also James, *Society, Politics and Culture,* 445–47.

27. Margaret Dowling, "Sir John Hayward's Troubles over his Life of Henry IV," *Library* 11 (1930):212–24; S. L. Goldberg, "Sir John Hayward, 'Politic' Historian," *Review of English Studies* 6, n.s. (1955):233–44.

28. *The Letters of John Chamberlain,* ed. McClure, 1:70.

29. *Stationers' Register,* ed. Arber, 3:677–78.

30. For analysis of revisions, see Kathleen Tillotson, "Drayton and Richard II: 1597–1600," *Review of English Studies* 15 (1939):172–79.

31. *CSP, Dom, 1598–1601,* 449. See also 539–40.

32. *The Works of Francis Bacon,* ed. James Spedding, Robert L. Ellis, and

Douglas D. Heath (Boston, 1860–64), 13:341. Cited in Leonard F. Dean, "Sir Francis Bacon's Theory of Civil History-Writing," *ELH* 8 (1941):161–83.

33. *CSP, Dom, 1598–1601,* 567.

Chapter Four

1. Sir John Hayward, *An Answer to the First Part of a certaine Conference, concerning Succession* (London: Simon Waterson & Cuthbert Burbie, 1603), A3v.

2. This dedication first appeared before *The Barons Warres* (1603) but was reprinted as the dedication to *Legends* (1619) where it appears in the standard edition (2:381).

Drayton engaged in a line-by-line revision of many passages in *The Barons Warres* for 1619. The 1603 version can only be reconstructed by moving between the 1619 edition printed in volume 2 of the standard edition and volume 5 (Tillotson) where textual variants are cited. Because this is a chronologically organized study, I prefer 1603 readings when they differ from the 1619 copy text. No stanza numbers are given with the variants in Tillotson; consequently, the 1619 stanza number is cited parenthetically in the text along with the line numbers; adjusted readings are designated "Tillotson" to indicate the need to consult the variants in volume 5.

3. See Stephen Greenblatt, *Renaissance Self-Fashioning, from More to Shakespeare* (Chicago: University of Chicago Press, 1980).

4. For Lucan's influence, see Anthony LaBranche, "Drayton's *The Barons Warres* and the Rhetoric of Historical Poetry," *Journal of English and Germanic Philology* 62 (1963):82–95; and LaBranche, "Poetry, History, and Oratory: The Renaissance Historical Poem," *Studies in English Literature* 9 (1969):1–19.

5. For Daniel's historical thought and references to earlier studies, see D. R. Woolf, "Community, Law and State: Samuel Daniel's Historical Thought Revisited," *Journal of the History of Ideas* (1988):61–83; Clark S. Hulse, "Samuel Daniel: the Poet as Literary Historian," *Studies in English Literature* 19 (1979):55–69.

6. Richard Niccols, *A Winter Nights Vision* in *A Mirrour for Magistrates* (London: Felix Kyngston, 1610). Niccols inserted his additions in the 1586 edition of *A Mirrour for Magistrates,* ed. John Higgins; hereafter signatures are cited parenthetically in the text.

7. Hardin, *Michael Drayton,* 41–45. *Poems of Michael Drayton,* 2 vols., ed. John Buxton (London: Routledge & Kegan Paul, 1953), 2:707–8. Kathleen Tillotson thinks *Mortimeriados* has "an enchantment," lacking in "the more responsible and competent" *The Barons Warres* (45). C. S. Lewis dismisses all of Drayton's historical verse except for *Englands Heroicall Epistles* as adding little to his reputation. Of *The Barons Warres,* he says "no historical estimate should deter us from saying that this is bad, bad work" (*English Literature in the Sixteenth Century* [Oxford: Clarendon Press, 1954], 532–33, esp. 533).

8. Appendix 2, Jonson, *Poems,* ed. Parfitt, 462, 478, lines 56–57; 637.

9. Both Buxton (ed., *Poems,* 1:192–94) and Tillotson (177–81) offer identifications based on annotated contemporary copies of *The Owle.*

10. For discussion of James's interest in divine poetry, see Lily B. Campbell, *Divine Poetry and Drama in Sixteenth Century England* (Cambridge: Cambridge University Press, 1959), 74–92.

11. Hardin, *Michael Drayton,* 1–9, 93–94.

12. On subversion as a convention of the ode, see Paul H. Fry, *The Poet's Calling in the English Ode* (New Haven: Yale University Press, 1980), 30–36.

13. *Calendar of the Manuscripts of the Most Honourable, The Marquess of Salisbury (1605),* ed. M. S. Giuseppi (London: His Majesty's Stationery Office, 1938), 17:291. In June 1605 Lucy alludes to Goodere when thanking Cecil for doing her a favor.

14. See chapter 1, n. 27. See also *The Returne from Parnassus* (1601) extracted in *Elizabethan Critical Essays,* 2 vols., ed. G. Gregory Smith (Oxford: Clarendon Press, 1904), 2:401.

Chapter Five

1. For the relation of *Poly-Olbion* to Drayton's literary ambition, see Parker Duchemin, "'Barbarous Ignorance and Base Detraction': The Struggles of Michael Drayton," *Albion* 14 (1982):118–38.

2. Quotations from *Poly-Olbion* refer to volume 4 of the standard edition; references are cited parenthetically with the number of the song followed by line numbers, e.g., (2.3–4). Songs 1–18 were published in 1612; songs 19–30 were published in 1622.

3. Hardin, *Michael Drayton,* 129.

4. For analysis of the engraving, see Margery Corbett and Ronald Lightbown, *The Comely Frontispiece: The Emblematic Title-Page in England, 1550–1660* (London: Routledge & Kegan Paul, 1979), 152–61.

5. For the philosophical implications of this metaphor, see Leonard F. Barkan, *Nature's Work of Art: The Human Body as Image of the World* (New Haven: Yale University Press, 1975).

6. Richard Helgerson, "The Land Speaks: Cartography, Chorography, and Subversion in Renaissance England," 327–61, in *Representing the English Renaissance,* ed. Greenblatt.

7. G. M. D. Howat, *Stuart and Cromwellian Foreign Policy* (New York: St. Martin's Press, 1974), 1–20.

8. Norbrook, *Poetry and Politics,* 102–6; Julia Briggs, *This Stage-Play World* (Oxford: Oxford University Press, 1983), 152.

9. Scholarship on influences on *Poly-Olbion* is too lengthy to be more than suggested. For a recent survey and analysis of topographical studies, see Stan Mendyk, "Early British Chorography," *Sixteenth Century Journal* 17 (1986):459–81; and William H. Moore, "Sources of Drayton's Conception of *Poly-Olbion,*" *Studies in Philology* 65 (1968):783–803.

10. For more on Leland, see James P. Carley, "John Leland's *Cygnea Cantio:* A Neglected Tudor River Poem," *Humanistica Lovaniensia* 32 (1983):225–41.

11. For connections between antiquarian research and politics, see Kevin Sharpe, *Sir Robert Cotton, 1586–1631: History and Politics in Early Modern England* (Oxford: Oxford University Press, 1979); Linda Van Norden's "The Elizabethan Society of Antiquaries," Ph.D. diss., University of California, Los Angeles, 1946; Van Norden, "Sir Henry Spelman on the Chronology of the Elizabethan College of Antiquaries," *Huntington Library Quarterly* 13 (1949–50).

12. Letter dated 10 July 1618, printed in Richard Parr, *The Life of James Ussher* (1686), 65. Cited in Helgerson, "The Land Speaks," 343.

13. John Selden, who prepared the notes for *Poly-Olbion,* disagreed with his historical interpretation. For an indication of the complexity of naming and classifying early peoples, see Susan Reynolds, "What Do We Mean by 'Anglo-Saxons'?" *Journal of British Studies* 24 (1985):395–414.

14. See I. Gourvitch, "The Welsh Element in the *Poly-Olbion:* Drayton's Sources," *Review of English Studies* 4 (1928):69–77; and Robert R. Cawley, "Drayton's Use of Welsh History," *Studies in Philology* 22 (1925):234–55.

15. For a valuable contribution, see Retha M. Warnicke, *William Lambarde, Elizabethan Antiquary* (London: Phillimore, 1973).

16. Richard Verstegan [Richard Rowland]'s *Restitution of Decayed Intelligence* (1605) paid tribute to the Old English language and to the Germanic tribes as the principal ancestors of the English nation. In song 4 Drayton's discussion of the Germanic identity of the Saxons and Normans seems indebted to the *Restitution* (369–412).

17. For a revision of the court and country division, see Kevin Sharpe, *Criticism and Compliment: The Politics of Literature in the England of Charles I* (Cambridge: Cambridge University Press, 1987), 1–53.

18. On *Poly-Olbion* as an idealized pastoral, see Stella P. Revard, "The Design of Nature in Drayton's *Poly-Olbion,*" *Studies in English Literature* 17 (1977):105–17.

19. Barbara C. Ewell, "Drayton's *Poly-Olbion:* England's Body Immortalized," *Studies in Philology* 75 (1978):297–315, 302.

20. For studies relating ideas and literary structure, see Wyman H. Herendeen, *From Landscape to Literature: The River and the Myth of Geography* (Pittsburgh: Duquesne University Press, 1986), 289–306; and Grundy, *Spenserian Poets,* 128–42. On the relationship between the two parts of *Poly-Olbion* (1612, 1622), see P. G. Buchloh, *Michael Drayton: Barde und Historiker, Politker und Prophet,* Kieler Beiträge zur Anglistik und Amerikanistik, bd. 1 (Neumünster: K. Wachholtz Verlag, 1964), 223–34; and Hardin, *Michael Drayton,* 61–66.

21. Paula Johnson, "Michael Drayton, Prophet without Audience," *Studies in the Literary Imagination* 11 (1978):45–55; cf. Grundy, *Spenserian Poets,* 132.

22. Samuel Daniel, *Poems and Defence of Ryme,* ed. Arthur Colby Sprague (Cambridge: Harvard University Press, 1930), 79. In *Musophilus* (1599) lines

336 through 390 concern Stonehenge; in later versions Daniel deletes lines 343 through 390.

23. For Drayton's use of the alexandrine, see Parker Duchemin, "Drayton's *Poly-Olbion* and the Alexandrine Couplet," *Studies in Philology* 77 (1980):145–60.

Chapter Six

1. Helgerson, *Self-Crowned Laureates,* 168–79, 254–57.

2. References to all works in this chapter are to volume 2 of the standard edition. Volume 2 reprints these works as they appeared in the 1619 folio, not in the order of their publication. Prefatory material is cited parenthetically by page number, poetry by line number.

3. Anne Barton, "Harking Back to Elizabeth: Ben Jonson and Caroline Nostalgia," *ELH* 48 (1981):701–31.

4. Tillotson, 15; Lewis, *English Literature in the Sixteenth Century,* 496; and Grundy, *Spenserian Poets,* 111.

5. For discussion of Drayton and Marlowe, see Grundy, "'Brave Translunary Things,'" 501–10.

6. Tillotson, 137. Tillotson has also provided a finding list based on first lines, giving sonnet numbers as well as dates of earlier editions (325–28).

7. For the influence of the drama and Donne, see F. Y. St. Clair, "Drayton's First Revision of his Sonnets," *Studies in Philology* 36 (1939):40–59; for Shakespeare's influence, see Katharine M. Wilson, *Shakespeare's Sugared Sonnets* (New York: Barnes & Noble, 1974); for Petrarch's importance as a model, see Carol T. Neely, "The Structure of English Renaissance Sonnet Sequences," *ELH* 45 (1978):359–89.

8. Rosemond Tuve, *Elizabethan and Metaphysical Imagery: Renaissance Poetic and Twentieth-Century Poetics* (Chicago: University of Chicago Press, 1947), 69–70.

9. Walter R. Davis, "'Fantastickly I Sing': Drayton's *Idea* of 1619," *Studies in Philology* 66 (1969):204–16.

10. Lewis, *English Literature in the Sixteenth Century,* 497.

11. Robert Shafer, *The English Ode to 1660: An Essay in Literary History* (Princeton: Princeton University Press, 1916), 82–91; on French influences, see Anthony LaBranche, "The 'Twofold Vitality' of Drayton's *Odes,*" *Comparative Literature* 15 (1963):116–29.

12. D. S. J. Parsons, "The Odes of Drayton and Jonson," *Queen's Quarterly* 75 (1968):75–84.

13. For Drayton's revisions in relation to Spenser, see Catherine A. Ackerman, "Drayton's Revision of *The Shepheards Garland,*" *College Language Association Journal* 3 (1959):106–13.

14. Alice S. Miskimin, *The Renaissance Chaucer* (New Haven and London: Yale University Press, 1975), 242–55.

15. For a study of fame in the Renaissance, see Edwin B. Benjamin, "Fame, Poetry, and History," *Studies in the Renaissance* 6 (1959):64–84.

Chapter Seven

1. For use of terms *epistle* and *elegy,* see D. J. Palmer, "The Verse Epistle," in *Metaphysical Poetry,* ed. D. J. Palmer and Malcom Bradbury, Stratford-upon-Avon Studies, 11 (New York: St. Martin's Press, 1970), 72–99; and Francis White Weitzman, "Notes on the Elizabethan Elegie," *PMLA* 50 (1935):435–43.

2. My discussion is indebted to the excellent analysis of *The Battaile of Agincourt* by Hardin, *Michael Drayton,* 70–72.

3. On Drayton's disillusionment, see Joan Rees, "Hogs, Gulls, and Englishmen: Drayton and the Virginian Voyages," *Yearbook of English Studies* 13 (1983):20–31.

4. On the Caroline historical epic, see Homer Nearing, *English Historical Poetry (1599–1641)* (Philadelphia: University of Pennsylvania Press, 1945), 178–90.

5. *Explorata: or Discoveries,* in Jonson, *Poems,* ed. Parfitt, lines 3,383–84, 456–58.

6. Raymond Jenkins, "The Sources of Drayton's *The Battaile of Agincourt,*" *PMLA* 41 (1926):280–93.

7. For comparisons with Herrick, see Floris Delattre, *English Fairy Poetry* (London: Henry Frowde, 1912), 148–57; Katherine M. Briggs, *The Anatomy of Puck* (London: Routledge & Kegan Paul, 1959).

8. Sir Philip Sidney, *A Defence of Poetry,* ed. Jan van Dorsten (1966; Oxford: Oxford University Press, 1975), 24.

9. Warren W. Wooden, "Michael Drayton's *Nimphidia:* A Children's Classic?" in *Children's Literature of the English Renaissance,* ed. Jeanie Watson (Lexington: University of Kentucky Press, 1986), 88–96.

10. Raymond Jenkins, "Drayton's Relation to the School of Donne, as Revealed in the *Shepheards Sirena,*" *PMLA* 38 (1923):557–87; J. William Hebel, "Drayton's Sirena," *PMLA* 39 (1924):814–36 (Hebel identifies Sirena as Anne Goodere and Olcon as Jonson); and Jenkins, "Drayton's Sirena Again," *PMLA* 42 (1927):129–39.

11. *Proceedings and Debates of the House of Commons in 1620 and 1621* (Oxford, 1766), 2:292–93. Cited from Patterson, *Censorship and Interpretation,* 44.

12. For the possibility that *The Muses Elizium* was presented as an entertainment at Dorset's family home, see Geoffrey Hiller, "Drayton's *Muses Elizium:* A New Way Over Parnassus," "*Review of English Studies* 21 (1970):1–13.

13. C. S. Lewis, *English Literature in the Sixteenth Century,* 535. Grundy, *Spenserian Poets,* 96–98. For an excellent study that pursues Drayton's substitution of the term *nymphal* for eclogue, see William A. Oram, "*The Muses Elizium:* A Late Golden World," *Studies in Philology* 75 (1978):10–31. For a study relating *The Muses Elizium* and Herrick's fairy poetry, see Barbara Ewell, "The Aesthetics of Fairy

Pastoral in Drayton's *The Muses Elizium,*" *South Central Bulletin* 42 (1982):131–33. For the view that the poem is not entirely golden, see Hardin, *Michael Drayton,* 127–36.

14. Tillotson suggests that Drayton, like the old satyr, found asylum with the Dorset family (220), as does Hardin (*Michael Drayton,* 131). For the argument that *The Muses Elizium* supports pure poetry, see Leah Jonas, *The Divine Science: The Aesthetics of Some Representative Seventeenth-Century Poets* (New York: Columbia University Press, 1940), 47–79.

15. Hardin, *Michael Drayton,* 129. See also Hardin's essay suggesting that sections of *Poly-Olbion* were adapted for use in *The Muses Elizium,* "The Composition of *Poly-Olbion* and *The Muses Elizium,*" *Anglia* 86 (1968):160–62.

Chapter Eight

1. For a biography, see Mary Hobbs, "Drayton's 'Most Dearely-Loved Friend Henery Reynolds Esq.,'" *Review of English Studies* 24, n.s. (1973):414–28.

2. James Clay Hunt, "The Elizabethan Background of Neo-Classic Polite Verse," *ELH* 8 (1941):273–304. James A. Means, "Drayton and Pope: An Unrecorded Parallel," *Notes and Queries* 26, n.s. (1979):23.

3. For this social context, see Arthur F. Marotti, *John Donne, Coterie Poet* (Madison: University of Wisconsin Press, 1986), 3–24.

4. Jonson, *Poems,* ed. Parfitt, lines 179–84, 466.

5. Bernard Weinberg, *A History of Literary Criticism in the Italian Renaissance,* 2 vols. (Chicago: University of Chicago Press, 1961), 1:198, cited in Hulse, *Metamorphic Verse,* 96–97.

6. Grundy, "'Brave Translunary Things,'" 501–10.

7. Thomas Lodge, *The Complete Works of Thomas Lodge,* 4 vols., ed. Edmund W. Gosse (1883; New York: Russell & Russell, 1963), 3:5; hereafter cited parenthetically in the text.

8. John Weever, *Epigrammes* (1599), ed. R. B. McKerrow (1911; Stratford-upon-Avon: Shakespeare Head Press, 1922), 28.

9. Guilpin, *Skialetheia,* ed. Carroll, 90.

10. Meres, *Palladis Tamia,* ed. Allen, 75.

11. Russell Noyes, "Drayton's Literary Vogue since 1631," *Indiana University Studies* 22 (Bloomington: Indiana University Press, 1935), 3–23.

12. Alwin Thaler, "Sir Thomas Browne and the Elizabethans," *Studies in Philology* 28 (1931):87–117; and Hans Gottlieb, "Robert Burton's Knowledge of English Poetry," Ph.D. diss, New York University, 1937.

13. Edward Phillips, *Theatrum Poetarum Anglicanorum: Containing the Names and Characters of All the English Poets from the Reign of Henry III. to the Close of the Reign of Queen Elizabeth,* revised by Samuel Egerton Brydges (Canterbury: J. White, 1800), 262–71.

14. Earl R. Wasserman, *Elizabethan Poetry in the Eighteenth Century* (Urbana: University of Illinois Press, 1947), 4; and Pat Rogers, "Drayton

Modernis'd: An Augustan Version of *Englands Heroicall Epistles*," *English Studies* 53 (1972):112–23.

15. For a discussion of Drayton's influence on the genre, see Gillian Beer's wide-ranging and suggestive "Our unnatural Novice: The Heroic Epistle, Pope, and Women's Gothic," *Yearbook of English Studies* 12 (1982):125–51.

16. W[alter] B[arker] Watkins, *Johnson and English Poetry before 1660*, Princeton Studies in English, 13 (Princeton: Princeton University Press, 1936), 85–110.

17. For supplemental information on influence, see the annotated bibliography by James Harner, *Samuel Daniel and Michael Drayton: A Reference Guide* (Boston: G. K. Hall, 1980), 147–302.

18. Frederick E. Pierce, "Blake and Seventeenth Century Authors," *Modern Language Notes* 39 (1924): 150–53.

19. Jared R. Curtis, "William Wordsworth and English Poetry of the Sixteenth and Seventeenth Centuries," *Cornell Library Journal* (1966):28–39.

20. For Coleridge's annotations of Drayton, see Hartley Coleridge, "Drayton," in his *Essays and Marginalia* (London: Edward Moxon, 1851), 2:3–4; and *Coleridge's Miscellaneous Criticism*, ed. Thomas Middleton Raysor (Cambridge: Harvard University Press, 1936).

21. Claude L. Finney, "Drayton's *Endimion and Phoebe* and Keats's *Endymion*," *PMLA* 39 (1924):805–13.

22. E. H. Meyerstein, "A Drayton Echo in Tennyson," *Times Literary Supplement*, 2 June 1950, 341; and Richard Hooper, "The metre of Tennyson's *In Memoriam*," *Notes and Queries* 46 (1872):338.

23. Edwin P. Whipple, "Minor Elizabethan Poets," *Atlantic Monthly* 22 (July 1968):26–35; and his "Minor Elizabethan Poets," in *The Literature of the Age of Elizabeth* (Boston: Fields, Osgood, 1869), 221–49.

24. Helgerson, "The Land Speaks," 360–61.

25. Amy Lowell, *John Keats*, 2 vols. (Boston: Houghton Mifflin, 1929), 1:79, 329–39; 563; and Sidney Colvin, *John Keats: His Life and Poetry* (New York: Charles Scribner's Sons, 1917), 167–72; 174–75.

26. Helgerson, "The Land Speaks," 360–61; and Norbrook, *Poetry and Politics*, 211–45.

Selected Bibliography

PRIMARY WORKS

Editions

Minor Poems of Michael Drayton. Edited by Cyril Brett. Oxford: Clarendon Press, 1907.

Poems of Michael Drayton. 2 vols. Edited by John Buxton. Cambridge, Mass.: Harvard University Press, 1953.

The Works of Michael Drayton. 5 vols. Edited by William Hebel (with Kathleen Tillotson and Barnard Newdigate). Oxford: Shakespeare Head Press, 1931–41; corrected edition, Oxford: Basil, Blackwell, & Mott, 1961. The four-volume standard edition was prepared by J. W. Hebel; volume 5 containing the notes was completed by Kathleen Tillotson and Bernard Newdigate. For the corrected 1961 edition, Bent Juel-Jensen has revised the bibliography, originally prepared by Geoffrey Tillotson.

SECONDARY WORKS

Bibliographies

Hardin, Richard F. "Michael Drayton." In *The Popular School,* edited by T. P. Logan and D. S. Smith. Lincoln: University of Nebraska Press, 1975.

Harner, James L. *Samuel Daniel and Michael Drayton: A Reference Guide.* Boston: G. K. Hall & Co., 1980.

Books

Buchloh, P. G. *Michael Drayton: Barde und Historiker, Politiker und Prophet.* Kieler Beiträge zur Anglistik und Amerikanistik, Bd. 1. Neumünster: K. Wachholtz Verlag, 1964. Discusses Drayton's biblical and secular history.

Elton, Oliver. *Michael Drayton. A Critical Study.* 1905; New York: Russell & Russell, 1966. Romanticized appreciation of Drayton's life and works.

Grundy, Joan. *The Spenserian Poets: A Study in Elizabethan and Jacobean Poetry.* London: Edward Arnold, 1969. Interprets Drayton as a successor to Spenser.

Hardin, Richard F. *Michael Drayton and the Passing of Elizabethan England.*

Lawrence: University of Kansas Press, 1973. Excellent critical study concentrating on Drayton's odes.

Newdigate, Bernard. *Michael Drayton and His Circle.* 1941; Oxford: Basil Blackwell for the Shakespeare Head Press, 1961. Biographical study of Drayton's patrons and friends.

Books and Parts of Books

Buxton, John. *A Tradition of Poetry.* New York: Macmillan, 1967. Influenced by the Newdigate biography.

Campbell, Lily B. *Divine Poetry and Drama in Sixteenth Century England.* Cambridge: Cambridge University Press, 1959. Useful comments on divine poetry in early seventeenth century.

Fry, Paul H. *The Poet's Calling in the English Ode.* New Haven: Yale University Press, 1980. Comments on subversion in Drayton's odes.

Helgerson, Richard. *Self-Crowned Laureates.* Berkeley and Los Angeles: University of California Press, 1983. Supplies interesting social context.

Herendeen, Wyman H. *From Landscape to Literature: The River and the Myth of Geography.* Pittsburgh: Duquesne University Press, 1986. Strong on ideas and literary form.

Hulse, Clark. *Metamorphic Verse: The Elizabethan Minor Epic.* Princeton: Princeton University Press, 1981. Useful discussion of Drayton's complaints and legends.

Lewis, C.S. *English Literature in the Sixteenth Century Excluding Drama.* Oxford History of English Literature. Oxford: Clarendon Press, 1954. Still useful as a critical touchstone.

Lytle, Guy Fitch, and Steven Orgel, eds. *Patronage in the Renaissance.* Princeton: Princeton University Press, 1981. Useful social background.

Norbrook, David. *Poetry and Politics in the English Renaissance.* London: Routledge & Kegan Paul, 1984. Suggestive discussion of Drayton as Jacobean critic.

Patterson, Annabel. *Censorship and Interpretation: The Conditions of Writing and Reading in Early Modern England.* Madison: University of Wisconsin Press, 1985. Seminal discussion of the impact of censorship on aesthetics.

Sharpe, Kevin. *Sir Robert Cotton, 1586–1631: History and Politics in Early Modern England.* Oxford: Oxford University Press, 1979. Useful background on the Society of Antiquaries.

————. *Criticism and Compliment: The Politics of Literature in the England of Charles I.* Cambridge: Cambridge University Press, 1987. Reexamines court and country divisions.

Warnicke, Retha M. *William Lambarde, Elizabethan Antiquary.* London: Phillimore, 1973. Fine study of antiquarian scholarship.

Whigham, Frank. *Ambition and Privilege: The Social Tropes of Elizabethan*

Courtesy Theory. Berkeley: University of California Press, 1984. Useful on rhetoric of clientage.

Articles

Ackerman, Catherine A. "Drayton's Revision of *The Shepheards Garland.*" *College Language Association Journal* 3 (1959): 106–13. Suggests his revisions moved in the direction of greater specification and smoothness.

Barton, Anne. "Harking Back to Elizabeth: Ben Jonson and Caroline Nostalgia." *ELH* 48 (1981):701–31. Supplies useful context for those who lived through the reigns of Elizabeth I, James VI and I, and Charles I.

Benjamin, Edwin B. "Fame, Poetry, and History." *Studies in the Renaissance* 6 (1959): 64–84. Comments on *Robert of Normandy.*

Bristol, Michael D. "Structural Patterns in Two Elizabethan Pastorals." *Studies in English Literature* 10 (1970): 33–48. Analyzes the structure of Vergil's pastoral eclogues and Drayton's imitation of that form in *Idea The Shepheards Garland.*

Campbell, Lily B. "The Use of Historical Patterns in the Reign of Elizabeth." *Huntington Library Quarterly* 1 (1938): 135–67. Useful background on parallels between Richard II and Elizabeth.

Carter, Katherine D. "Drayton's Craftsmanship: The Encomium and the Blazon in *Englands Heroicall Epistles.*" *Huntington Library Quarterly* 38 (1975): 297–314. Describes the rhetorical structure of *Englands Heroicall Epistles.*

Corbett, Margery, and **Ronald Lightbown.** *The Comely Frontispiece: The Emblematic Title-Page in England, 1550–1660.* London: Routledge & Kegan Paul, 1979. Chapter 13 concerns the frontispiece of *Poly-Olbion.*

Davis, Walter R. "'Fantastickly I sing': Drayton's *Idea* of 1619." *Studies in Philology* 66 (1969):204–16. Stimulating description of *Idea* (1619) as a comic sequence.

Duchemin, Parker. "'Barbarous Ignorance and Base Detraction': The Struggles of Michael Drayton." *Albion* 14 (1982):118–38. Comments on *Poly-Olbion* in Drayton's career.

————. "Drayton's *Poly-Olbion* and the Alexandrine Couplet." *Studies in Philology* 77 (1980): 145–60. Metrical analysis.

Ewell, Barbara C. "The Aesthetics of Fairy Pastoral in Drayton's *The Muses Elizium.*" *South Central Bulletin* 42 (1982):131–33. Comments on Herrick and Drayton.

————. "Drayton's *Endimion and Phoebe:* An Allegory of Aesthetics." *Explorations in Renaissance Culture* 7 (1981): 15–26. Interprets *Endimion and Phoebe* as allegory of poetic inspiration.

————. "Drayton's *Poly-Olbion*: England's Body Immortalized." *Studies in Philology* 75 (1978):297–315. Shows that the world's body is a controlling metaphor unifying theme and structure in *Poly-Olbion.*

————. "From Idea to Act: The New Aesthetics of Drayton's *Englands Heroicall*

Epistles." *Journal of English and Germanic Philology* 82 (1983): 515–25. Places *Englands Heroicall Epistles* in the context of Drayton's career.

————. "Unity and the Transformation of Drayton's Poetics in *Englands Heroicall Epistles.*" *Modern Language Quarterly* 44 (1983):231–50. Argues for a major shift in Drayton's aesthetic principles in the *Epistles.*

Fish, Stanley. "Authors-Readers: Jonson's Community of the Same." In *Representing the English Renaissance,* edited by Stephen Greenblatt, 231–64. Berkeley: University of California Press, 1988. Enlightening discussion of effect of patronage system on tone.

Friedrich, Gerhardt. "The Genesis of Michael Drayton's Ode 'To the Virginian Voyage.'" *Modern Language Notes* 72 (1957):401–406. Discusses Richard Hakluyt, compiler of travel literature as a source.

Grundy, Joan. "'Brave Translunary Things.'" *Modern Language Review* 59 (1964): 501–10. Perceptive analysis of the implications of the term "clear" for Drayton's poetic theories.

Hardin, Richard F. "The Composition of *Poly-Olbion* and *The Muses Elizium.*" *Anglia* 86 (1968):160–62. Suggests unused passages of *Poly-Olbion* were incorporated in *The Muses Elyzium.*

————. "Convention and Design in Drayton's *Heroicall Epistles,*" *PMLA* 83 (1968):35–41. Compares *Englands Heroicall Epistles* with Ovid's *Heroides.*

Hebel, J. William. "Drayton's 'Sirena.'" *PMLA* 39 (1924): 814–26. Discusses figures in Drayton's eighth eclogue and identifies Sirena, Olcon, the swineherds, and shepherds of *Sirena* as Anne Goodere, Jonson, Tribe of Ben, and Spenserians.

————. "The Surreptitious Edition of Michael Drayton's *Peirs Gaveston.*" *Library* 4, 4th ser. (1923), 151–55. Suggests publication occurred when Drayton was not present to read proof.

Helgerson, Richard. "The Land Speakes: Cartography, Chorography, and Subversion in Renaissance England." In *Representing the English Renaissance,* edited by Stephen Greenblatt, 327–61. Berkeley: University of California Press, 1988. Essential reading for *Poly-Olbion* and Drayton's politics.

Hiller, Geoffrey G. "Drayton's *Muses Elizium:* A New Way over Parnassus." *Review of English Studies* 21 (1970): 1–13. Argues that *Muses Elizium* was written to be presented as an entertainment and that Robert White's *Cupid's Banishment* was an important source.

Jenkins, Raymond. "Drayton's Relation to the School of Donne as Revealed in 'The Shepherd's Sirena.'" *PMLA* 38 (1923): 557–87. Interprets *The Shepheards Sirena* as Drayton's defense of the Spenserians against the school of Donne.

————. "Drayton's 'Sirena' Again." *PMLA* 42 (1927):129–39. Replies to Hebel's identification of Olcon as Jonson.

LaBranche, Anthony. "Drayton's *The Barons Warres* and the Rhetoric of Historical Poetry." *Journal of English and Germanic Philology* 62 (1963):82–95. Describes influence of Lucan and use of rhetorical figures in *The Barons Warres*.

————. "Poetry, History, and Oratory: The Renaissance Historical Poem." *Studies in English Literature* 9 (1969): 1–19. Rhetorical discussion of *The Barons Warres* and *Englands Heroicall Epistles*.

————. "The 'Twofold Vitality' of Drayton's Odes." *Comparative Literature* 15 (1963): 116–29. Compares the ways in which Drayton and Ronsard use classical models.

Lewalski, Barbara. "Lucy, Countess of Bedford: Images of a Jacobean Courtier and Patroness." In *Politics of Discourse: The Literature and History of Seventeenth-Century England,* edited by Kevin Sharpe and Steven Zwicker, 52–77. Berkeley: University of California Press, 1987. Excellent biographical analysis of the patroness whom Drayton spurned.

Moore, William H. "Sources of Drayton's Conception of *Poly-Olbion.*" *Studies in Philology* 65 (1968): 738–803. Supplies detailed survey of influences on *Poly-Olbion*.

Nearing, Homer, Jr. *English Historical Poetry, 1599–1641.* Philadelphia: University of Pennsylvania Press, 1945. General discussion of historical verse with positive assessment of Drayton.

Noyes, Russell. "Drayton's Literary Vogue since 1631." *Indiana University Studies* 22 (Bloomington: Indiana University Press, 1935):3–23. Only uses number and frequency of scholarly editions to judge reputation and influence.

Oram, William A. "*The Muses Elizium:* A Late Golden World." *Studies in Philology* 75 (1978):10–31. Suggestive study of *Muses Elizium* as a statement about imaginative literature.

Parsons, D. S. J. "The Odes of Drayton and Jonson." *Queen's Quarterly* 75 (1968): 75–84. Compares Jonson and Drayton and sees Drayton's revisions as moving toward the grace and smoothness of Caroline verse.

Petronella, Vincent F. "Double Ecstasy in Drayton's *Endimion and Phoebe.*" *Studies in English Literature* 24 (1984): 87–104. Reads *Endimion and Phoebe* as a description of Neoplatonic ecstasy.

Rees, Joan. "Hogs, Gulls, and Englishmen: Drayton and the Virginian Voyages." *Yearbook of English Studies* 13 (1983):20–31. Study of Drayton's pessimism.

Revard, Stella P. "The Design of Nature in Drayton's *Poly-Olbion.*" *Studies in English Literature* 17 (1977): 105–17. Discusses pastoral and political themes as organizational devices.

Short, R[aymond] W. "Ben Jonson in Drayton's Poems." *Review of English Studies* 16 (1940):149–58. Proposed identifications hotly contested in *Review of English Studies* 16 (1940) by Percy Simpson, 303–5, and by Kathleen Tillotson, 305–6.

Taylor, Dick. "Drayton and the Countess of Bedford." *Studies in Philology* 49 (1952):214–28. Presents bibliographical evidence that printers were responsible for retaining dedications to the Countess of Bedford up to the 1619 folio.

Tillotson, Kathleen. "Drayton and Richard II: 1597–1600." *Review of English Studies* 15 (1939):172–79. Shows that Drayton revised *Englands Heroicall Epistles* for political reasons.

_____. "Drayton and the Gooderes." *Modern Language Review* 35 (1940): 341–49. Important biographical article on Drayton's service in Thomas Goodere household.

_____. "The Language of Drayton's *Shepheards Garland*." *Review of English Studies* 13 (1937):272–81. Discusses his revisions for the 1606 edition.

_____. "Michael Drayton as a 'Historian' in the 'Legend of Cromwell.'" *Modern Language Review* 34 (1939), 186–200. Examines use of sources and themes.

_____. "Spenser's 'Aetion.'" *Times Literary Supplement,* 7 February 1935, 76.

West, Michael D. "Drayton's 'To the Virginian Voyage': From Heroic Pastoral to Mock-Heroic." *Renaissance Quarterly* 24 (1971): 501–6. Discusses inconsistency that results from combination of diverse modes in one poem.

Index